Eight Brief Lessons on Life

Eight Brief Lessons on Life

T. Byram Karasu

HAMILTON BOOKS
Lanham • Boulder • New York • Toronto

The Rowman & Littlefield Publishing Group, Inc.
4501 Forbes Boulevard
Suite 200
Lanham, Maryland 20706
Hamilton Books Acquisitions Department (301) 459-3366

Unit A, Whitacre Mews, 26-34 Stannary Street,
London SE11 4AB, United Kingdom

Printed in the United States of America

British Library Cataloging in Publication Information Available
Library of Congress Control Number: 2018956521
ISBN: 978-0-7618-7085-2 (pbk. : alk. paper)
ISBN: 978-0-7618-7086-9 (Electronic)

™ The paper used in this publication meets the minimum requirements of American National Standard for Information Sciences—Permanence of Paper for Printed Library Materials, ANSI Z39.48-1992

Contents

Acknowledgments

I am grateful to a number of individuals who contributed to the realization of this book. Specifically, I want to thank Julie Kirsch, Vice President/Publisher at Rowman and Littlefield, for her exceptional dedication to this project; Mikayla Mislak, Assistant Acquisitions Editor; Meaghan Menzel, Assistant Production Editor, for skillfully pulling together all facets of the book's production; Theresa Phillips, for typesetting so efficiently, and Kathi Ha, for creating a beautiful cover that captures the spirit of the book. I thank both Joyce Faust, of Art Resource of New York, and Julie Zeftel, Senior Manager of Rights and Permissions at the Metropolitan Museum of New York for facilitating permission for me to use my cover image from the Metropolitan Museum's collection. I am appreciative of Yasmin Tariq for all the work associated with the preparation of the manuscript. I am indebted to Robert Swanson: a book of this kind is made so much more accessible by an index, and I could not have had a more competent ally in this process than Robert.

I am especially indebted to my wife, Sylvia R. Karasu, M.D., Clinical Professor of Psychiatry at Weill Cornell Medicine for her scholarly contributions, editorial rewritings, and her enduring love. This book could not have come to fruition in its current form without her.

Introduction

Uncommon Common Sense

There was once an old country priest who had listened to his parishioners' confessions for many decades. This priest summed up what he had learned about human nature in two statements: "First of all, people are much more unhappy than one thinks. . . and second, there is no such thing as a grown-up person."[1] Poignantly, the priest never defined happiness nor did he explain what he meant by "grown-up," but the implication is that these two concepts are somehow related, if not the same: the path to happiness goes by way of being grown-up.

While unhappiness is easy to define, happiness is not definable *a priori*. We know that obsessively focusing on attaining happiness not only fails to bring it about but leads to people's missing their own presence. "Grown-up" is also not definable because it is not a fixed state; there are degrees of being grown-up. Growing-up is an improvisational process. In fact, we all "grow-up" or "not," while living. We make our way by going, but we should not be like Tristan, who travelled on the sea without oar or rudder, making his way by playing his harp. We must at least know our destination, i.e., adulthood, even though we may not know how to get there.

Our fundamental essence requires organizing our mind into a cohesive narrative of self. We learn by osmosis and by transmuted internalizations from our families, schools, and society that inundate us with information, but not necessarily with knowledge, and leave us often at certain stages of an adult developmental arrest. Life's maturational knowledge is gained through experiences, especially what we do with these experiences, and how we struggle to come up with answers to some basic questions: Who am I? Or even, am I? How best to live or even why to live? Am I well-grounded or even, half-glued? What is the essence of love, marriage, work, religion? What are the principles of living and dying? These are not merely esoteric questions that just generate a philosophical dysphoria. They are essential in finding remedies for an inner disquietude that we all experience and in searching to establish harmony within ourselves. "Aldous Huxley referred to this as the 'perennial philosophy,' that is, the philosophy that remains the same at all times, in all places under all circumstances and for all people."[2]

As human beings, we are unique and universal. In Broadway lingo, plays don't change; only actors do. Actors (people) are unique and plays (lives) are universal. We all experience immediate or time- released traumas; we all participate in real and subjective impasses; we all suffer from anxiety resulting from various forms of real or anticipatory disruptions; we all get depressed from actual and imaginary losses. All human activities, joys, sorrows, pain, pleasure, desires, fears, etc. mirror each other in their basic elements. In the Jungian sense, we humans have irreducible psychological templates. We are not always sure of what it is that we are really looking for, but we know all the time that we haven't found it yet. Spira expressed this nameless, formless, barely discernible feeling, "There is a dissatisfaction in me, but I am not sure exactly what I am dissatisfied with. There is a longing in me, but I am not sure what I am longing for."[3] At other times, we feel we are almost there, but never there. Like the mythological Tantalus[4], we are condemned to reach yearningly for that so-near fruit that recedes anew with each fresh attendant grasp.

We all have indistinct outlines of our life's trajectory; we all kind of fiddle with life. As we grow up, we have to make sense of our lives. We need to attend to the business of getting a grip on life, and our place in it. We need to formulate a much clearer guiding principle of our existence and learn the art of living. These principles need not be expressed *via negativa*. "How much nonsense humans will suffer for the sake of making sense of their lives,"[5] says Benjamin Moser.

Like Jung, Rupert Spira asks the ultimate questions: "'Is there any element of subjective experience that is universal or shared by all?' or 'If the mind only ever knows its own contents, is there any element of the mind's knowledge or experience that is common to all minds?' That knowledge alone can qualify as absolute truth and, therefore that knowledge alone can serve as the basis of a unified humanity."[6]

Only in such an accumulated knowledge base, can we make sense of our lives and find positive guideposts. *Eight Brief Lessons* provides these guideposts. Its lessons evolve from a highly condensed distillation of thousands of years of wisdom—*uncommon common sense*. This is not just a means to virtue; it is also a means to joyfulness. It provides a template for the essence of being, becoming a grown-up, and living a joyful and successful life.

All advice-givers commit some form of fallacy and are not immune from inherently self-limiting conjectures. With full awareness of that, am I still presenting myself as a "know it all," a *man of wisdom*? Samuel Johnson reportedly once said that he was accused of being a wise man, 'All I can tell you, I have good judgment; how does one have good judgment? By having lots of experiences. And how does one get lots of experiences? By not having good judgment.'

Now, in my eighties, I have also had "lots of experiences," and, as told about graduates of French Haute Ecole, "I know everything and nothing else."

NOTES

1. André Malraux, *Anti-Memoirs*, trans. Terence Kilmartin (New York: Henry Holt and Company, 1990), 1.
2. Rupert Spira, *The Nature of Consciousness Essays on the Unity of Mind and Matter* (Oxford: Sahaja Publications, 2017), 4.
3. Rupert Spira, *The Nature of Consciousness Essays on the Unity of Mind and Matter*, 62.
4. Thomas Bulfinch, *Bullfinch's Mythology* (New York: Penguin Group, 2014), 223.
5. Benjamin Moser, "Patriarch and Pariah," *The New York Times Book Review*, July 6, 2014: https://www.nytimes.com/2014/07/06/books/review/american-crucifixion-by-alex-beam.html.
6. Rupert Spira, *The Nature of Consciousness Essays on the Unity of Mind and Matter*, 9.

Lesson One

Love

Live a "felt" life, and be alive

The first lesson is love: in fact, it could have been the only lesson. Without love, the rest of the lessons are irrelevant.

There are many forms of love and all of them are magical. There is loyalty-sustained and imprinted filial love for family members. There is affection-sustained friendship love that entails a fondness and appreciation of another. There is physical desire-sustained erotic love and its most exalted version, romantic love. These four forms of love are "differentiated object" loves; they target a person or a group; they are specific and object-driven. Then there is spiritual love—the love of all beings. Spiritual love is undifferentiated; it targets no one and everyone. It is just love. Buddha says that ultimate love is love with no object.[1]

Love in all its variations is a universal phenomenon; it is the primary organizer of mind and a marrow of life that anchors all relationships. Victor Frankl, in his chapter on logotherapy in *Man's Search for Meaning* speaks of finding meaning in life "by experiencing something—such as goodness, truth and beauty… (and) last but not least, by experiencing another human being in his very uniqueness—by loving him."[2] Love is the only way to grasp the innermost core of another being; it is also the only way to grasp our own core of being.

Romantic love—that raucous ascension, is the most popular and celebrated in all languages, races, and ages. It is associated with beauty, youthfulness, and fueled by the most powerful emotion: aching longing. Passionate love brings about an ever escalating endowment of the beloved, with denial of the self. What the Zen master says about the divine is almost true in passionate love: "In the existence of your love, I became non-existent."

Love is the pain of being truly alive. This pain in love is compounded with an equally powerful and agonizing sentiment: "to be longed for."[3] This longing to be longed for, of course, is beyond a lover's ability to bring about. You can neither demand, nor buy it. Love is not a substance that you give or take; it is not a tradable commodity. It is a felt referent, rather than a conceptual referent. If forced, it is a kind of "felt cognition." The only currency for passionate romantic love is passionate love itself. Such passion cannot be faked. In contrast to love itself, both intercourse and orgasm can be faked and/or can be artificially generated.

This passionate love is intensely associated with the pleasure bond. It is a poetic condensation of libidinal urges, wrapped in romantic camouflage. Its recipients project an unequalled hedonistic gloss. Ironically, actual sexual intercourse of lovers is utterly selfish and exigent; lovers are hardly interested in each other's subjective experiences, and that is what makes their lovemaking so powerful and satisfying. Even in the movies, lovemaking scenes are presented with such a mutual selfish urgency. The heightened excitement of the partner is what excites the other. Lovers rarely talk while having sexual intercourse, and rightly so, for language preempts the experience. The more we are concerned about anything objective, especially about another, the less exciting sex gets. The famous behaviorist Skinner reportedly told the following vignette to an audience: Two behaviorists are making love; afterwards one asks the other one: "It was very good for you; how was it for me?"

Passionate love has no rules or guide books. It is *id-ridden* and thus generates many excesses: triangulated jealousies, social transgressions, destructive and self-destructive behaviors. What seems to be all that unfair, if not insane, to innocent onlookers is totally fair to those participants lost in the inner lawlessness of love. Passionate love is a death-daring attachment, an unconscious trap that only a rare lover can escape.

> In his book *A Legacy of the Heart*, Wayne Muller speaks of a monkey trap in Asia:
>
> First, a coconut is hollowed out and attached by a rope to a tree. Then, a small hole is made at the bottom of the coconut and some sweet food is placed inside. The hole in the bottom is just big enough for the monkey to slide his open hand into the coconut, but not big enough for a closed fist to pass through. The monkey smells the sweets, reaches in with his hand to grab it, and then, with the food clenched tightly in his fist, he is unable to withdraw it. The clenched fist cannot pass through the opening. When the hunters come, the monkey becomes frantic, but it cannot get away. There is nothing keeping the monkey captive except the force of his own attachment. All he has to do is open his hand, let go, and he is free. Even so, it is a rare monkey that manages to escape.[4]

After all is said and done, human beings are incomprehensible: it is more so for lovers. They are at their best and at their worst when in love. William Godwin is at his best in his declaration of his love to Mary Wollstonecraft: "When I make love, it shall be with the eloquent tones of my voice, with dying accents, with speaking glances (through the glass of my spectacles), with all the witching of that irresistible, universal passion…When I make love, it shall be in a storm, as Jupiter made love to Semele, and turned her at once to a cinder."[5]

Passionate love is a sort of febrile agitation of mind, an aching lust spewing out from the biological furnace of the body and ransacking its habitation. It has all elements of delusion and impractical preoccupation with the lover, including her/his past to the exclusion of all other concerns; it tends to be ruthless and paranoid; it has an obsessive desire to possess the other person's past. Such engrossment is not satisfied with the love of the lover; puzzlingly, it aims at appropriation of the lover, if not his/her annihilation. Love even confounds the Bible: "There are [many] things which are too amazing for me, four which I don't understand: The way of an eagle in the air, the way of a serpent on a rock, the way of a ship in the middle of the sea, and the way of a man with a maiden."[6]

The lowest order of love, sex, can be just for physical pleasure, within or without emotional connections. In comparison to passionate love, its rudiments of illusions dissolve in immediacy. The indulgence in sex with multiple partners is an impersonal and pathological quest of the self in others, as portrayed by Don Juan. Trachtenberg, in his book *The Casanova Complex*, writes that 18th century Casanova "made a virtual career of seducing women."[7] "To Casanova, every woman was a potential paramour," says Trachtenberg, and in his *Memoirs*, Casanova wrote, "I am neither tender nor gallant nor pathetic. I am passionate."

Such excesses thin the soul, leading to sexual incontinence and to moral relativity.

Sex is a physiological act, similar to other physiological functions of the body. In all animals, sex serves procreation. It is the same in humans, especially at the subcortical level of our brain. The evolution of the brain in humans, that is, its cortical development, however has added many other dimensions to sex: entertainment, anxiety reduction, power play, expression of aggression, emotional control of partner, a displacement of obsession, and frequently an alternate or substitute addiction. Such sex interferes with the growth of love, so much that its roots remain weak and are easily torn up.

The pleasure aspect of sex is best experienced in passionate love wherein a mutual longing transforms lovers into an ecstatic state of abandon. Frequently such passionate love ends by its loss: either when one of the lovers loses the intensity and/or its inter-cognitive resonance of their love, or when one becomes too clingy with a disintegrating anxiety of losing the lover. That is one of the most serious mistakes in emotional life. You lose what you cling to, and not just in love. Everyone needs to study the art of letting go.

It is difficult to sustain passionate love partly because such an exaltation of another demands mystery of and a psychological unfamiliarity with the lover. Any shedding light on the lover will dissolve the mystery and will dissipate that boundless ecstasy. What is desired cannot be all and always so desirable. What we really love is how we feel when in love. That is, we love our desire and not what is desired.

Sex researchers identify the half-life of passion at the four-year mark.[8] "Love begins as a sonnet, but it eventually turns into a grocery list," says Joel Achenbach in "Homeward Bound."

"Therefore, you need someone with whom you can go to the supermarket."[9] In passionate love, lovers with uncanny erotic intelligence gaze at each other; for it to survive they need to look out and together in the same direction. They need to cultivate the same unforced, natural emotional intimacy to save the relationship from the decline of sexual attraction and passion. It may take about two years for such an emotional intimacy and affectionate love to develop between lovers, provided that the couple remains physically close and sexually reciprocative.[10]

While passionate love is also a power and control struggle (wherein who loves less is the more powerful), the opposite is true in affectionate love, wherein the stronger partner subordinates. Affectionate love translates poetry into prose. Affectionate love is primarily asexual; the deeper it gets, the more it desexualizes the relationship. That doesn't mean that affectionate couples don't have sex; they have "good-enough sex." But that sex is less a longing for ecstatic merging than for satisfying physical and psychological needs for self and/or for the partner—another expression of caring.

Affectionate love is a soft descent; it has a filial origin. It is where we all begin and end up in our relationships, if we are so fortunate. This is the love that is felt most deeply and enduringly when it is lost. Affectionate love is our emotional home, our anxiety-reducing sanctuary; in contrast to the *fortissimo* of passionate love, affectionate love is expressed *pianissimo*, noiselessly. It is with our mothers (or a maternal person) that we first experience that affectionate love. Obviously, the fetus is a part of the mother, who continues to experience the child as her extension even after the birth. The love of the mother for her child isn't the love of someone else; it is like the love of the self. A child, if so loved, feels emotionally attuned to, without any need for reciprocation. A mother knows the inner life of the child intuitively and attends to its needs while often muting her own. A person's well-glued, coherent "sense of self" develops within such a context. In all our lives we carry a mix of highly pixelated memories of this early childhood feeling and try to bring them into focus in our contemporary relationships. In that sense, love is our relentless search for completion of our primordial selves—a healthy yearning, not like the pathological quest of the self in others.

Our self continues to be formed and cultivated in relational contexts, no matter how indifferent we may seem to be. Even the primitive disinterestedness of cats plays out within complex relationships. The original relational context—parental mirroring and shaping—eventually gives way to a peer relationship: lovers, spouses, and especially friends.

While all other relations are time-limited, real friendship with time gets only deeper and more meaningful. Epicurus considered friendship absolutely necessary provided that it has no utilitarian impositions. Friendship brings a state of lucidity, if it is among the self-sufficient who are reliant on each other but not dependent. Such a friend is an alternate self.

A good friend, a really good friend, is our first affectionate relationship outside the family. It is the second imprinting phase in our lives. We learn many things from friends that we cannot learn from our parents. Many other qualities such as virtue and loyalty get reinforced within good and healthy friendships. Rewording Primo Levi, each of us bears the imprint of friends we met along the way and carries their traces.[11]

The master of neoclassical English poetry, Alexander Pope, had these words around the time of his death, according to Samuel

Johnson's biography of Pope: "There is nothing that is meritorious but virtue and friendship; and indeed, friendship itself is only part of virtue."[12]

We all have a number of associates, colleagues, and acquaintances, but a few real friends.

A friend is someone with whom we can be totally transparent; we may be criticized, even laughed at, but never diminished or rejected. We are accepted as we are, even though certain changes may be wished for. Actually, the only way to bring about desired changes is to accept that person as is.

Acquaintances with various degrees of intimacy are the most common form of a relationship. Such relationships are maintained by mutual interests, such as through businesses, jobs, or by common interests in social life. These relationships tend to have a secondary agenda. We should not expect total loyalty or permanency from such agenda-based relationships. There is a French peasant saying: "Cow dies, partnership ends." Expecting fallibility from such relations is less likely to create disappointments. Genuine loyalty is like genuine love; it is not transactional.

In contrast to passionate love, affectionate love is less selective. Its needs being met are as important as who meets them. Affectionate love is not exclusive: if you can love one person, you can love many. Except if you choose one as your "soulmate." "Soulmateness" is a highly distilled form of affectionate love between two, commonly unrelated people. Soulmates cross their individual boundaries; they resonate with each other cognitively and emotionally in perfect harmony, as if they are extensions of each other. This is not a pathological symbiosis: it is the most exclusive club, difficult to find, and almost impossible to join. You may search but searching may not be the best way of finding a soulmate. Cultivation of condensed empathy for others eventually finds its reciprocating target. Nietzsche says "From love of man one occasionally embraces someone in random,"[13] provided that these two highly empathetic beings spend a great deal of time being together and cheer each other through crises and adversities.

Affectionate love gently lifts our spirit, for it is not jealous, impatient, or intense; it is kind, optimistic, and non-judgmental. "Love is patient" says the Bible.[14] Affectionate love is healthy love. It is not obsessive, hysterical, or possessive; it respects privacy, and the space and separateness of the other person. Affectionate love is to say, "I am sorry."

Existence is inherently dissatisfying due to its non-permanency. Love in all its forms carries a sense of permanency, real or illusionary. As such, it makes life worth living and gives an overriding meaning to all life's lesser meanings. Only by giving and receiving love can we live a "felt life." Without love, we are lifeless.

> The mind has a thousand eyes. And the heart but one;
> Yet the light of a whole life dies.
> When love is done.[15]

In an ascending ladder, all love, from animalistic carnal lust, where tyranny of senses dictates, to divine madness of passionate love, from cognitive emotional love of friends and family members, to Plato's attainment of wisdom, (the seed of theological visions), makes life worth living. Lovelessness is radical aloneness. A lover partakes of the beloved. The more you love, the more you will be connected to others but more importantly to yourself. But first, you must love yourself—a benign healthy self-love—only then can you love others.

Socrates believed that the yearning for love is essentially about possession of goodness and beauty. Plato qualified that acquisition by saying that it must be permanent. Both philosophers were saying that we all are yearning and searching for immortality in the forms of goodness and in the beauty of love. In Plato's *Republic* (Book VI), Socrates and his companions discuss the importance of beauty, "Do you think that the possession of all other things is of any value if we do not possess the good? Or knowledge of all other things if we have no knowledge of beauty and goodness?"[16] They set the stage for the next concept, spiritual love. All love is good and beautiful, but it is only perfected when the loved object is perceived within an ever-enlarging context—spiritual love. Such love unfolds from loving a specific object towards loving an all-encompassing context itself.

Spiritual love is not *Agape*—God's love. The love of God is irreducible—axiomatic, belonging to an apodictic category of self-evidency. Love without an object, i.e., spiritual love, of course, partakes in love of God as well. It is a different kind of self-seeking from other loves, for it seeks equanimity in goodness, benevolence in goodwill. Objectless love is not divine love. It is not self-sacrificing concern for the fallen. It is selfless, but not sacrificial; it is a compassionate presence in the world but not actively engaged in its expressions. It demands neither obedience, compliance nor exaltation. It is as it is.

Both love with object and love without object are involuntary. But the love of object (person, thing) is self-affirming; it is utilitarian, particular and reluctantly accepts substitutes. Love without object is self-muting, non-utilitarian, non-particular and welcomes all substitutes as originals.

In object love, love is expressed from the lover. In objectless love, love flows through the person, effortlessly. Object loves are dualistic: i.e. I love you or it. There is the loving subject and the loved object. Dualistic love is an important stage in the development of the self. Even the love of God is dualistic in the early stages of mind that conceptualizes God as a separate being rather than as its absoluteness. Objectless love is monistic: there is no separate I, you or it. We are all one—a transcending stage of spirituality wherein God and "you" are a single entity.

A logical mind would be hard pressed to accept all this objectless love—spiritual love. In fact any kind of love may not seem logical: a fantasy of platonic writers and poets. But it is real, and in fact, neuroscience has advanced to the level of pointing to a biological location of love—dopamine intoxication—in the brain's nucleus accumbens.

Object love is an epiphenomenal entity, defined by human interactions. Objectless love—spiritual love—is the hardest to define. It doesn't lend easily to descriptive, rational language. This love, the ultimate love, wants nothing for itself and rewording spiritual teacher Francis Lucille, it is benevolent indifference to itself. It is conceptually an irrational and epistemologically imprecise, if not null, proposition. But if you witness the sun shining and the rain descending upon all, you may consider the possibility of a serene existence where you may be infused within a seemingly infinite love. You'll be awakened, like Buddha, in a minor key. Incidentally Buddha means "one who is awake."

A sudden enlightenment rarely occurs in a quantum leap; it commonly arrives in drawn-out attenuated forms. You'll begin to see the hidden beauty and goodness in other beings and things and experience, even if only flickering hints, a joyful resolve in your own benevolence.

In his book, *Works of Love*, Kierkegaard tells the parable of two artists: one artist travels the world and cannot find any face with "such perfection of beauty" that he wanted to paint. The other artist, who stays within his "little circle of men," says, "…I have not found a face so insignificant or so full of faults that I still could not discern in it a more beautiful side and discover something glorious." How sad it would be, continues Kierkegaard, if the demands of love "make it evident that none of us is worth loving, (but) instead…(to be) able to find some lovableness in all of us…"[17]

It is said that love is blind because it has a better sight. Spiritual love has the ultimate sight: the love that permeates everything and for no reason. Spiritual love is a state of mind, a way of being. It negates all objective counterpoints.

NOTES

1. Gil Fronsdal, "The Buddha's Teachings on Love." https://www.insightmeditationcenter.org/books-articles/articles/the-buddhas-teachings-on-love/. Retrieved July 11, 2018.
2. Victor E. Frankl, "Logotherapy in a Nutshell," in *Man's Search for Meaning: An Introduction to Logotherapy*. (Cutchogue, NY: Buccaneer Books, Inc, 1992), 115.
3. R.D. Laing, *The Politics of Experience* (New York: Pantheon, 1967), 74.
4. Wayne Muller, *Legacy of the Heart The Spiritual Advantages of a Painful Childhood* (New York: Fireside Book, 1993), 140.
5. William Godwin and Mary Wollstonecraft, *Goodwin & Mary*, ed. R.M. Wardle, (Lawrence: Bison Books, 1977) 4–5, 8.

6. Proverbs 30:18–20.

7. Peter Trachtenberg, *The Casanova Complex: Compulsive Lovers and Their Women*. (New York: Poseidon Press,1988), 31–32; note #32, page 278.

8. Helen E. Fisher, *Anatomy of Love: The Natural History of Monogamy, Adultery, and Divorce* (New York: Norton, 1992), 10.

9. Joel Achenbach, "Homeward Bound," in *Here Lies My Heart: Essays on Why We Marry, Why We Don't, and What We Find There*, foreword by Amy Bloom, ed. Deborah Chasman and Catherine Jhee (Boston: Beacon Press, 1999), 50–56.

10. Cindy Hazan and Debra Zeifman "Sex and the Psychological Tether" in *Attachment Processes in Adulthood*, ed. Kim Bartholomew and Daniel Perlman. Vol 5, *Advances in Personal Relationships*, 151–78. (London: Jessica Kingsley, 1994).

11. Primo Levi, "To My Friends," in *The Mirror Maker* (Schocken Books, 1998), 5.

12. Alexander Pope in *Johnson's Life of Pope,* ed. Samuel Johnson and Peter Peterson (London: Macmillan and Co., Limited 1899), 71.

13. Friedrich Nietzsche, *Beyond Good and Evil: Prelude to a Philosophy of the Future*, ed. Rolf-Peter Horstmann and Judith Norman, trans. Judith Norman (New York: Cambridge University Press, 2002), 72.

14. 1 Corinthians 13:4.

15. Francis William Bourdillon, "The Night Has a Thousand Eyes," in *The Night Has A Thousand Eyes and Other Poems* (Cambridge: Little, Brown, and Company, 1899), 13.

16. Plato, *Republic,* Book VI: 190–223, trans. Benjamin Jowett. With an Introduction and Notes by Elizabeth Watson Scharffenberger George Stade Editorial Director, (New York: Barnes and Noble Classics, 2004), 214.

17. Søren Kierkegaard,"Our Duty to Love Those We See," in *Works of Love,* trans. Howard and Edna Hong, (New York: HarperPerennial/ ModernThought, 2009), 156–157.

Lesson Two

Work

Synchronize yourself with your work, and be successful

Our work is one of the defining characteristics of who we are, how we relate to the world, and how we relate to ourselves. "The love that goes to your work comes back as self-love"[1] says Thomas Moore. Work is one of our prisms. For Freud, at least as Erikson relates, happiness is reached simply by "*Arbeiten und Lieben*" ("to work and to love")[2]. The Sufis say work is faith—dip your bread in your sweat. Work is *liber mundi*, a "book of the world," say Catholic monks—work is life literacy. "*Laborare est orare* (Work is worship)."[3] But they all imply reasonably successful work. Occasional failures are fine, if not desirable, but they do not consider chronic failures as the source of happiness.

There may be a multiplicity of influences, but success at work primarily depends on whether you love what you are doing. The Bengali poet Rabinandrath Tagore says "I grew tired of the road when it took me here and there. I married the road in love when it took me Everywhere."[4] Furthermore, work must be suitable for your skills and knowledge—a kind of dwelling in your element. All work demands certain basic skills; there is really no such thing as "unskilled labor." A young construction worker must know how to walk on steel beams. Computer literacy is expected in most jobs, even from a beginner. Of course, every expert was once a novice, and expertise for a specific skill may require on-the-job learning.

There is also the question of temperament. Unfortunately, people sometimes choose their careers for certain prestige, power, and money, and often independent of their suitability for those jobs. Whether your brain is lateralized to right or left and whether your corpus callosum is firing well in both directions are important to know. Do you have a digital mind that employs discrete bits or an analogue one that operates on continuous linearity?

Of course, you should cultivate aspirations, but you must know the basic rules of your aspired career. For example, in music, sound and structure require adherence to an exactness of 1/3 of a second (e.g. 16 notes with mm-60). Then, and only then you can hum. We cannot all be musicians or cannot be innately suitable for careers like nursing or sales. While certain empathy for suffering is desirable for nurses, facile encounters with strangers are necessary for salesmanship. You must know your skills and potentials and build on them. That is not to say you cannot be trained for those dispositions, but that will be like learning a second language—it is hard and rarely fluent.

We need to succeed somehow, to be competent at something, to be a master at even some minor skills in order to feel good about ourselves. Our self-esteem is highly dependent on feeling relevant, needed, valued and appreciated. That requires, of course, earning our merit without stagnation. All other compensations will follow once merit is earned. Any mastery is a lifelong apprenticeship. Think of a black belt judo master, who wanted to be buried in a white belt, so that he can go on learning in eternity.

Success, i.e., mastery, should not be confused with illusionary perfection. Good is good enough. Upon completing the universe, God pronounced it "very good"[5] not perfect. You may strive for greatness, but do not underestimate the value of good, basic usefulness. Leonard Cohen, the famous poet and musician, reportedly was once asked by a producer who wasn't sure whether he could make money out of this reticent poet; he said, "I know you are great; but are you any good?"

The point of reference for success should not be your parents or others, but yourself. By standards of "shoulds" we all fail. The point of reference is being true to yourself. If your innate disposition is not suitable for a certain type of work, you will not succeed in spite of any singular determination. Whatever you do is another manifestation yourself. You may approximate, but ultimately you must synchronize your work with yourself in order to reach your goals. Such synchrony is best displayed where one cannot tell the singer from the song.

Equally important, you must come to terms with your limitations and/or learn how to get around them, if you are so determined. We are all tirelessly confronted with our limitations. Accept your shortcomings and see their virtues as the Bible advises: "I will rather glory in my weaknesses"[6] Caesar covered his defects with laurels. But do not let your limitations define you. Some of these limitations are given to you at birth but it is what you do with them that counts, whether those are limitations of your intelligence, your health, your family background, or all other inequalities and privileges.

Your circumstances may not be reflecting your real potential. Musical geniuses are born to totally tone-deaf parents, scholars to illiterate parents. Anthony de Mello tells the following story:[7] A farmer found an abandoned eagle's nest and in it was an egg that was still warm. He took the egg back to his farm and laid it in the nest of one of his hens. The egg hatched and the baby eagle grew up along with the other chickens. It pecked about the farmyard, scrabbling for grain. It spent its life within the yard and rarely looked up. When it was very old, one day it lifted up its head and saw above it a wonderful sight—an eagle soaring high above in the sky. Looking at it, the old creature sighed and said to itself, "If only I'd been born an eagle." So, even if you are surrounded with chickens, always aspire to be an eagle; in fact you may be one. Our genes are multigenerational.

Intuitionistic cognition is a fallacy; an impotent cultivation of subjectivity has no place in business. Neither successes nor failures are overnight occurrences. They are usually the results of hard work and cultivation of certain objective behavioral patterns.

In our imprinting stages of development (~ages 0-11 years), we have two nodal points that seed our characterological traits: oedipal and pre-oedipal stages with their own conflicts and deficits. If unresolved, the former creates various forms of neuroses that present themselves with colorful rhetoric. The latter generates unwell minds that present colorless pseudo-neurotic states. People in both groups complain about their miseries, illnesses, losses, pains, bad luck and misfortunes with such a negative exuberance that you may suspect that they are getting vicarious pleasure from their misfortunes. They keep repeating their depressive stories so often that eventually they do get depressed for real. There is an Irish proverb: a man becomes a song he sings. Highly intelligent but neurotic or pseudo-neurotic people can even be self-destructive. It is that Medea phenomenon, i.e., a person can act against her better judgment. You need to recover from your imprinted conflicts and deficits, mute your negative noises from within and learn to sing positive, modest and benign, self-loving cheerful songs; but do not join a cult of self.

Independent of professional skills and dispositions, there are some generic and cultivatable psychosocial skills that contribute to any success. For example, listen, and listen attentively. In an old fable, a man spends days climbing to the top of a mountain where the Zen master lived. Finally, when he was allowed to be in the master's presence, the man asked: "Master, I have been on the road for weeks to see you and ask for some wisdoms of life." Master said: "Attention." The man, disappointed, asks, "Is that it? Can you say something more or just elaborate?" Master replied: "Attention, attention."

Whatever the job, you must be fully immersed and absorbed in it. You need to remain in the present, live in the "no-time," when children are playing for leisure and artists are having singular concentration for work. You need to focus, filter, reflect, and be responsive to minimum cues and respond accordingly. Do not speak more clearly than you think, and when you speak remain relevant and within the context. Conversational postulates demand that what you say has to be understandable even if you are a poet, and what you say has to have a clear relation to what the other person has just said. Dialectical relations are not linear, but progressively and cumulatively spiral, mediated by both directions.

Language is a tool of communication. In its highly elaborate forms, it tends to become the source of miscommunication. The

> first principle of communication is to respond to the other person's questions. Do not be self-referential. The Japanese proverb says, "You must send the message whether received or not." There is, however, another saying: "It is not enough to aim; you must also hit the target."[8]

Whatever we say is spoken representation of events, concepts, things, etc. It is easily misunderstood, at times preemptively and wrongly. Pick up minimum cues and calibrate a subtle latency of response. Some talk too much and say nothing just as some of our politicians, or worse, generate unnecessary predicaments. It is said that one can seldom listen his way into trouble. You can accomplish much just by being quiet, pleasant and agreeable. A man's *gravitas* emanates from the density of the unspoken. Be assertive but not aggressive and never transgressive. Taoism emphasizes strength in yielding. Sometimes you need to yield to overcome. Never complain or blame. The litany is an inner pollution. It is in the Bible: Do all things without murmurings and disputings.[9] Never accuse others. There is a Zen saying: When a man points a finger at someone else, three fingers are pointing back at himself. Try it, to help with your pre-reflective awareness.

Success comes by functioning as if everything depends on you; by having mini goals, by generating an energy of positive priming and leaning forward wholeheartedly. But do not become a zealot—a psychological disorder of the inexperienced. *Meden agan*—nothing in excess, is engraved on the Temple of Apollo.

You must patiently keep seeding even though nothing seems to be growing; suddenly those seeds will sprout. God didn't make the world in one day (the exact time lapse is seven!). You need to be steady, resilient, and patient. Drops also fill the pot. Says

Buddha: When you dig a well, there is no sign of water until you reach it, only rocks and dirt to move out of the way. Once you have removed enough of them, the water will start flowing.

You should not try to outdo others, but rather just outdo yourself. Do not seek an ego orgasm. Establish and present an inner stability; never generate crises. For some unfortunate people, the only sense of cohesiveness they attain is by identification with chaos. Be aware of such dysfunctional ways of relating.

Work in synchrony with others. You may hear a different drummer, but still keep the band in sight. You need to synchronize with the band (your job); the band will not synchronize with you. If there is no synchrony between the two, then you need to change either the job or yourself. There is an in old Jewish saying: if you cannot change the world, change yourself.

Realistic self-assessment is said to be a sellout, but commonly people tend to overestimate themselves and with a neurotic conviction and undervalue their assigned roles. We see that mostly in the offspring of wealthy parents who have Janusian grandiosity and low self-esteem. They are helicopter children, dropped at the mountaintop. They have to come down first and then learn how to walk up the mountain. Otherwise they'll end up being victims of their fortunes.

Do not expect work to meet all of your hopes and aspirations. As far as a job is concerned, there is no utopia. In fact, the word utopia is from ancient Greek *outopos*, meaning "no place."

You should not dismiss an assignment because it is below your skillset or because it is "meaningless" or "uninteresting." Very few things in life are inherently meaningful and interesting. Most things do become interesting once we get interested in them. The meaning of anything reveals itself only to those who are committed.

There is a story of a traveler who stops by a construction site and watches four workers in each corner breaking massive stones with enormous hammers. The traveler asks the first worker "What are you doing?" The man doesn't answer; he doesn't even lift his head to look up. The second man answers angrily "I prepare these damned mortars, a job suitable for hard labor prisoners!" The traveler approaches the third man with the same question. He looks content. "This is a really hard job" he says, "but it pays well, and I need to support my large family." The fourth man looks more serene; he dusts himself off, "Yes, sir, we are building a church." While all four men are doing the same job, their attitudes are so different. The first man who doesn't even bother to answer the traveler's question, is indifferent—a source of aloneness. The second man is breaking stones without any purpose or meaning—a source of anger and unhappiness. The third person has a limited purpose—a source of contentment. The fourth person is meaningfully engaged and identified with the project—a source of joyfulness.

Incidentally, the importance of even a humble "purpose" should not be underestimated. You cannot miss the inner glow of purposeful. They are the people who may not get up every morning with unbridled enthusiasm, but they get up.

The third man's explanation of why he has been doing that hard work is in some ways more functionally meaningful than an overendowed "abstract meaning in life." Looking for abstract meaning is an intellectual exercise that ends up in a meaningless and depressive impasse. The fruitlessness of such a search is best portrayed by Samuel Beckett's wife's question when he, looking full of despair, came home after a day's work: "No meaning again today, dear?"[10]

Purpose and meaning are byproducts of engagement in what one does—one's work, provided that the job is doable. No matter whether it is "meaning-endowed," the work must be doable by some realistic judgment. You don't want to face the predicament of the Norse God Thor, who tried to drain a goblet only to discover that it was connected with the sea.

You should not be excessively cautious or worry about making mistakes. The Bible says "He that observeth the wind shall not sow; and he that regardeth the clouds shall not reap."[11] Like in a chess game, in work, if not in life, mistakes are all there to be made, and you will make them. It is commonly recognized that errors and mistakes are the best teachers. But having too many teachers becomes boring! Most mistakes are related not to actions but to not anticipating the wake that they leave behind. They can be quite painful. Especially self-made calamities are difficult to survive. Independent and in spite of your best efforts, personal and professional failures may still occur. You need to be prepared to contain your losses, not to avoid painful feeling. Grief is a healing feeling. In fact, you may better by feeling worse.

Failure's most damaging effect is demoralization. Even the previously most self-confident and intelligent person, all of a sudden will feel less so, in fact, inadequate and helpless. Demoralization lowers motivation and distorts the perceptions of the person who sees even ordinary tasks of life, never mind the larger goals, as utterly insurmountable.

Eventually distorted perceptions contort the cognitive and executive skills of a person and leads him/her to draw incorrect, if not self-destructive, conclusions. Common incorrect conclusions are:

1. Being the only one who failed.
2. I am done; I can never recover.
3. I'll keep failing.
4. I am suffering; I cannot think about recovery right now—psychological inertia.

As to the first incorrect conclusion, you are not unusual; you are not the only one who failed. In fact, by a highly conservative estimate, failures outnumber successes by 10 to 1; the most successful people outrank the average person in failure by an even greater multitude. History is full of them. Steve Jobs was fired from Apple when he was a co-founder. Stephen King got over thirty rejections for his first novel *Carrie*. Arianna Huffington's run for California's gubernatorial race only got an abysmal 0.55 percent of the vote. Warren Buffet's initial acquisition of Berkshire Hathaway was a serious mistake. Churchill failed sixth grade and was defeated in every election until the age of 62. Bill Gates's first company Traf-O-Data, was a total failure. Lady Gaga was dropped by Island Def Jam Records! Oprah lost 80% of her assets with the colossal failure of her movie venture *Beloved*. Einstein was thought to be mentally handicapped by his teachers, and J. K. Rowling had many rejections before a publisher recognized the creativity of her *Harry Potter*.

The second incorrect conclusion: "I can never recover," is only true if you don't learn from your experience, if you do not pick up from where you failed and try to succeed again. Steve Jobs found another small company fittingly called *Next* which he later sold to Apple and he eventually became its CEO. Stephen King eventually became a bestselling author. Warren Buffet dumped everything from Berkshire Hathaway except its name and converted it into an investment firm. All of these individuals attributed their recovery from failures primarily to their certain mindsets: seeing failure as a preparation for success (S. Jobs), resetting her expectations (Oprah), using rejections as a tool to build resilience (S. King), considering failure as a stepping stone to success (B.

Gates), viewing her rejections as identification with some of her favorite writers (J.K. Rowling).

They are too modest not to mention certain personality traits that they all share: clarity of their minds, their work ethic, their persistence, and being undaunted in the face of adversities. They all took a certain perspective: they observed their failures as an event or events, single or multiple, but did not make the failure their state of mind: they did not generalize and internalize the "I failed" to "I am a failure."

That brings us to the third incorrect conclusion: "I am not lucky; I keep failing again and again in my field." First of all, a long run of bad luck is always suspicious. You can change your field like Arianna Huffington who gave up her political ambition after repeated failures and shifted to the publishing world, successfully. Or stay on course. But don't quit while you are behind, unless you are honestly a multi-untalented unfortunate.

You are expected to operate inside of your strength zone, but outside of your comfort zone. If you believe in your capacity and the feasibility of your endeavors, you are more likely to succeed eventually if you remain resilient. In the process, you need to formulate a personal narration of your perseverance and devotion in the face of repetitive failures. For example, "the more attempts one makes, the greater the chance of success." In fact, Thomas Edison, in his often cited attempts to develop light bulbs failed over 1000 times, Edison replied that he didn't fail 1000 times; it took him 1000 steps to invent a light bulb. Equally Dyson made over 5000 attempts before he succeeded in inventing the bagless vacuum cleaner. If Dyson quit at his 4999th and Edison at his 999th attempt, they would have been failures. Both demonstrated not only incredible perseverance but also an almost religious belief in themselves and their engagements.

Almost all significant individuals in the Bible experience horrific failures prior to their successes. Joseph was sold into slavery by his brothers because of his ambitions, even though they were only expressed in his dreams. Long before Freud, it was known that dreams don't lie. In Egypt, Joseph offended the powerful husband of a beautiful lady, for being subjected to her interest, and he was jailed. Job's ordeal is well-known. He failed and suffered spectacularly. Failures of Joseph and Job, especially Job, seem to stem from without. In the Bible there are also failures from within which are associated with the transgressive behavior of the individuals. David is the best example; he sexually abused Bathsheba and had her husband killed; he ignored his son's Ammon's rape of his half-sister. Peter, Gideon, and many others all made mistakes; they all had their own failures, and they all recovered.

The Bible attributes their recovery and ultimate successes to their work ethics, their loyalty, steadfastness, and their perseverance. They believed in their causes and their own identity.

The Bible is a very good textbook of psychology. Even the solutions presented in the Bible as to how to recover from failings, i.e., even hitting rock bottom, is the essence of all contemporary advice. For example, "Shake off the dust that is under your feet."[12] Rock bottom is the most solid foundation. Apostle Paul tells how he copes without lingering too long on past failures or problems: "One thing I do: forgetting the things which are behind, and stretching forward to the things which are before."[13]

The 4th incorrect conclusion that the brain makes, is "I am suffering; I cannot think of recovery right now." Yes, mistakes and failures are painful. Depending on their nature, they can be devastating. Some may come with public humiliations, others with personal guilt, regrets, and some others with private deprivation, or divorces, all of which inflict enormous damage. But this is the worst possible time for psychological inertia, or the worst time to throw in the proverbial towel. Boxing coaches urge boxers to keep fighting and not to pay attention to the audience. We tend to resonate with the reaction of others to our failure, more than we do from having failed.

So, what to do? First, set a time limit on self-pity and self-flagellation. Let's say a month, but not 24/7. You must take regular time off from wallowing. During this self-confrontation time, you must call it what it is and be totally self-transparent. No denial, no blaming others, no sugar-coating. You must look at the mistake squarely; what exactly happened, why it happened, what was my contribution, what was the contribution of others, and what contributions were indirectly my fault? Of course, there may be external contributions to failure that are totally out of our control, whereby we are simply a victim of circumstances.

At times, external contributions are related to mis-calibration on the trust/mistrust spectrum. There is a story of the Prophet Mohammed who was one day taking a stroll when he noticed that a Bedouin was leaving his camel untied, while heading towards the market. The Prophet asked him, "Why are you not concerned that your camel may just wander off while you are gone?' The Bedouin replied "I put my trust in Allah." The Prophet pulled the man toward him and whispered into his ear "Tie your camel first, then put your trust in Allah."[14] Although neither excessive suspicion, nor excessive trust is adaptive, and you may be better off to tie your camel.

The second step is setting down a plan to recovery. There is always a way out or a way through. You'll need to reframe the failure as an experience, like any other. A failure is rarely a life or death drama. Failure is supposed to be a teacher, not an undertaker. You must draw the line at your losses, whether physical, financial, or emotional. More importantly do not compound failure with another mistake in the process of trying to undo it. Casinos rely on gamblers' being primed to make even riskier bets to recover their losses, only to lose their shirts. The temptation to undo the mistake quickly without considering its potential consequences may compound the problem. Two wrongs don't make a right.

Rarely a single or a few mistakes may lead to major failures. In fact we usually fail in life at simply minor things. These mistakes usually have rigid boundaries, and they tend to be self-corrective. They become problematic if they are repetitive. It is curious that some people tend to repeat their mistakes. One would think that it should be enough to taste one drop of the sea to know that it is salty. It is in the Bible "As a dog that returns to its vomit, so is a fool who repeats his folly."[15] Making an unwanted approach to a colleague can be an interpersonal mistake, but repeating it is a pattern of behavior, that reflects some self-defining psychological aberration. We are what we repeatedly do, says Aristotle. While incalcitrant transgressions invite punishment, isolated personal mistakes—like a gambler's fallacy—need psychological help. The punishment for such personal mistakes is included in the mistake itself.

Wisdom of learning from mistakes is inconvertible, yet people take painstaking efforts to remain loyal to their mistakes. This is called "letting failure go to one's head." They perversely enjoy *capitis diminutio*—with a negative exuberance—and, in fact, have a certain subversive glee of satisfaction; in failing, it is like:

"I am a failure, I don't have to fail anymore." Roger Darlington once told the story of the late Rev. John King, who apparently talked about his days in San Quentin penitentiary with a kind of relief and contentment. He no longer had to be a "Reverend," but simply a prisoner.

To fail is to be human. The Bible reads: "Man who is born of a woman is of few days and full of trouble."[16] That means all of us. The only man who never made a mistake, says Theodore Roosevelt, is the man who never does anything.[17] That would be a meta-mistake.

No matter what field you are in, you must prepare yourself for potential failures. In fact, you can practice failing in small doses to gain some psychological immunity against larger and real ones. Very rarely is one's failure fatal. Short of that, a relative, if not full recovery, is the norm, ranging from adaptation to the new reality to even greater successes. Your real worth will remain unchanged even after a failure of public consequences. Once, when a motivational speaker, holding up a $100 bill, asked the audience who would like to have it, all hands went up. Then, he threw the bill on the floor and stomped on it with his dirty shoes. The speaker picked up the crumpled and soiled bill and asked the audience: "Now who would like to have this?" Again, all hands went up!

Young pilots are told at their first class that there are 16 ways to fall from the sky. As in Sophocles' *Oedipus Rex* wherein the culprit turns out to be the detective, all except for one relate to human errors. If you failed no matter what field you are in, it is 1/16 times as likely that it is related to your own mistake. There is a spectrum of personal mistakes. Common ones are operational i.e. risky deviation from the norm, careless inattention—auto-piloting—not knowing the subject well, and not considering consequences of your actions. Then, there are failures associated with the darker and deeper flaws of a person: a pathological sense of invincibility, invulnerability, infallibility and a sense of immunity. There is a difference between a semi-delusional belief in a cause and self-delusion.

Failures related to personal flaws are abject failures. We see those "falling heroes" in financial, sexual, and political arenas. They are tragic events. Such individuals would be better not to be isolated solo players. They would be better off to buttress themselves by working with a team. Team work, besides being a protective device, is a source of great successes. Short of poets, writers, and other creative people who are in fact in need of isolation, most will benefit in many ways from working with a team, especially if one is the leader—the lead goose. On his website, Roger Darlington relates the following story:

> Next autumn, when you see geese heading south for the winter, flying in a "V" formation, you might consider what science has discovered as to why they fly that way. As each bird flaps its wings, it creates uplift for the bird immediately following. By flying in a "V" formation, the whole flock adds at least 71 percent greater flying range than if each bird flew on its own.
>
> When a goose falls out of formation, it suddenly feels the drag and resistance of trying to go it alone and quickly gets back into formation to take advantage of the lifting power of the bird in front. [18]

Concrete recovery from failure must start independently from any psychological reactions by preparing a massive action plan. Think of a scenario where you fell from a paddleboat into a lake. Now, there is nothing else to feel, to think or to do except to get back to the boat, or swim to a shore. Real failure is not having failed, but how you react to it—not getting back to the boat.

First treat the failure as a problem, a serious one, a complicated dilemma; and recast it for a solution. Drain its venom; free your brain cells from useless obsessions; ruthlessly weed out all external contributions, if there are any. Stop bleeding, and whenever you return from a loss, it is a gain. If you are unable to reboot yourself, because you may be paralyzed with the fear of another failure, then find a mentor, a partner with whom to work.

Reset your goals and give a clear shape to your methods to achieve them; focus and practice those goals with total engagement. Expect new obstacles; prepare yourself for new surprises and even further failings. Formulate in your mind strategies, and be determined to overcome failings, should that happen. Meanwhile all the time, maintain self-monitoring. Our lives are shaped largely by our thoughts. Be clear about your intention, your end points. Do you want to be just successful or successful about something very specific? You must be able to focus simultaneously on the whole field with wide-angle attention and also focus on a specific matter with zoom-lens attention as well as shift back and forth. Generic success climbing may derail a person. There was a man who climbed such a ladder of success, only to discover that his ladder was put up against the wrong wall.

The most productive aspect of failures is in its helping to solidify your resilience. Some people have inherited resilience while others have to cultivate it. Resilience is a mixture of concrete acts and abstract attitudes—a philosophy of surviving. It is tenacity, an ability to take punches, and not stay there when hitting the floor. Thomas Edison's ten years' work on a storage battery was totally destroyed in a fire. His panicked son found him watching it serenely. Edison asked his son to calm down and witness this spectacular "show" which he may never see again. Later he said with the same repose, "Well now that all my mistakes burned up,

I can start anew." Within a few months, Edison delivered his first phonograph.

Resilience is self-efficacy, the ability to stand alone without waiting for someone to hold you up. Resilience is the ability to work in adversity, fully understanding and accepting the inequities of life. For the resilient, success is not the absence of failures, but the ability to deal with failures. Resilience is flexibility; it is swaying harmoniously in the winds of life without becoming uprooted—a healthy yielding. Resilience is adaptation to external forces, like a river, flowing over and around rocks.

Cultivation of resilience requires gaining a relative comfort with the uncomfortable. It is being inoculated to stress by repetitive exposure to adversities in life and plasticity training of your ventromedial cortex—the area in the brain that controls and regulates emotions. It is learning to have optimistic patience, taking a long view of life. Newly planted bamboo trees show no evidence of growth for the first year and will push only tiny shoots for the next five years. But eventually those shoots will grow one meter a day.

Ultimately resilience is equanimity, a possessing of a sense of well-being, even in view of the inevitable. A Zen master says if you are caught in a mousetrap eat the cheese. In the desolate Manzanar, the internment camp for those of Japanese descent after Pearl Harbor, only a few stones remain. Most of those stones are carved by its inhabitants with a Japanese saying *"Shikata ga nai—"nothing can be done."*[19] There is really nothing more they could have said. But they survived this ultimate adversity and in fact, most thrived. At times, resignation is the only option left for the resilient—*Zen-noire* wisdom.

Things in life are rarely as good or as bad as they seem to be. If anything, they are like the dances of Echternach (a town in

Luxembourg), where dancers advance 3 steps forward and 2 steps backward in their processions.[20] We all move forward stumbling and occasionally tripping and falling. If so, do not be afraid of hitting the bottom hard with optimistic toughness. That is the fastest way to come back to the surface. Ultimate success is recovering from a failure, and taking life on, again.

NOTES

1. Thomas Moore, *Care of the Soul: A Guide for Cultivating Depth and Sacredness in Everyday Life* (New York: Harper-Perennial), 187.
2. Sigmund Freud, quoted in Erik Erikson, *Identity and the Life Cycle* (New York: International Universities Press, 1968), 96.
3. Thomas Carlyle, *Past and Present* (Boston: Standard Publishing Company, 1898), 198.
4. Rabindranath Tagor as quoted by Deepak Chopra in Rupert Spira, *The Nature of Consciousness: Essays on the Unity of Mind and Matter* (Oxford: Sahaja Publications, 2017), xi.
5. Genesis 1:31.
6. 2 Corinthians 12:9.
7. Anthony de Mello, *Heart of the Enlightened: A Book of Story Meditations* (New York: Doubleday, 1991), 75.
8. Sylvia R. Karasu and T. Byram Karasu, *The Art of Marriage Maintenance* (New York: Jason Aronson, 2005), 89.
9. Philippians 2:14.
10. John Gardner, *Conversations with John Gardner* ed. Allan Chavkin (Jackson: University of Mississippi, 1990), 168.
11. Ecclesiastes 11:4.
12. Mark 6:11.
13. Philippians 3:13.

14. Tirmidhi (reworded), *Hadith on Reliance: Trust in Allah, but Tie Your Camel*, retrieved June 29, 2018. https://abuaminaelias.com/daily hadithonline/2012/11/17/hadith-on-reliance-trust-in-allah-but-tie-your -camel-and-give-regard-to-worldly-causes.

15. Proverbs 26:11.

16. Job 14:1.

17. Theodore Roosevelt, *The Oxford Dictionary of American Quotations*, 2nd Edition, ed. Hugh Rawson and Margaret Miner, retrieved July 11, 2018. http://www.oxfordreference.com/view/10.1093/acref/ 9780195168235.001.0001/acref-9780195168235

18. Roger Darlington: "A Sense of a Goose," retrieved July 11, 2018. http://www.rogerdarlington.me.uk/stories.html.

19. Melissa Hung, "Walking in Their Footsteps at a Former Japanese Internment Camp," National Public Radio. April 29, 2017, retrieved on July 11, 2018. https://www.npr.org/sections/codeswitch/2017/ 04/29/485574562/walking-in-their-footsteps-at-a-former-japanese-internment-camp.

20. "Dancing Procession of Echternach," The official portal of the Grand Duchy of Luxembourg, retrieved July 11, 2018. http://www .luxembourg.public.lu/en/le-grand-duche-se-presente/fetes-traditions/ procession-dansante/index.html.

Lesson Three

Belong

Expand your outer communion, and be grounded

Although there exists an *a priori* self, the sense of self is substantiated by being acknowledged—a kind of Descartes, or Hegel compromise. We all long to be known. In his book, *Wilhelm Meister's Apprenticeship and Travels*, Goethe has Wilhelm say that a poet receives (Book II, Chapter II) "…from nature, the right enjoyment of the world, the feeling of himself in others, the harmonious conjunction of many things that will seldom exist together."[1] In fact, existence is essentially co-existence. Although an adult should cultivate the capacity to be alone, he or she cannot live alone. This need for others is not just about physical survival, but also about a psychological one. Very few of us can survive by being alienated from our communities without succumbing to self–alienation. Like a boat we need at least two anchors to remain stable, and three are even better. The Bible says a "threefold cord is not quickly broken."[2] We cannot be cut off both from the supernatural order above—God—and from the natural order below—a congregation—and expect to survive. If we excommunicate ourselves, we will need to sustain and develop our own self-grounding philosophy. This is a tall order, and if at first you don't succeed, you'll be running above average.

In the broadest sense, belonging is a storytelling, in first person plural. The more complex the content of the story, the more it has the consequences of engaging emotions, thoughts, and actions. Religions provide the most complex stories. They are the opposite of Aristotelian teleology wherein goal-directedness simplifies life with its mechanical view of life, a form of truth, a naked reality—normality. Religion is normative, but it has nothing to do with "normality." It is about meaning rather than truth and offers a way to live in harmony.

Religion gets an unfair view because of being intertwined with the cosmological order of theology. But theology is one thing, and religion is another. Theology requires believing. One needs not believe in religion; one only needs to belong to it. If there is any believing in it, it comes with social osmosis, i.e. those repetitive *sui generis* practices in commune, especially as they relate to the "beyond." Nowhere is this more apparent than in funeral rites.

Religion offers a context to find meaning in life, not *the* meaning of life; that belongs to theology. Religion urges living a value-infused life and emotional alignment with a community, if not the world.

Belonging is a basic need: primarily it reinforces belonging to one's self; it infuses inner inquietude and anxiety tied to various types of disruptions in continuity; it infuses life with a sense where one is and where everything else is. It brings theology down to earth—the cosmological order simplified. There was an old monk working at the temple farm under the sun. A young monk asked him why he is working. He replied, "because I am here." The young monk continued, "Why work under the sun?"

The old monk said, "Because it is there." The reason we belong is because we are here, and we belong to religion because it is also here.

We all need moorings in a communal matrix, outside of our families. Jobs, associations, clubs and other organizations provide variant matrixes for present-time engagements. We should wholeheartedly engage in what is here and now—social relations with others to generate fun, laughter and a sense of lightness. Even the Bible notes, "Iron sharpens iron; so a man sharpens his friend's countenance."[3]

But our longing to belong is not only for the present, but also for the past and for the future. The orchestra score drives its value from the fact that it is anchored, read both vertically and horizontally at the same time. Such anchoring is only provided by a congregation, however real or illusionary. Ego psychology, developed by Erik Erikson, considers religion as a means by which people maintain a basic hope or trust in life in order to move from one stage of life to the next.[4] Belonging generates oxytocin, the hormone that fosters trust and interpersonal bonds. Rabbi Harold Kushner writes, "One goes to a religious service, one recites the traditional prayers, not in order to find God (there are plenty of places where He can be found), but to find a congregation."[5] Ministers hope that the congregation may lead them to God. The longtime director of a monastery once asked for what reason do people come to your monastery? He replied that everyone comes here for the wrong reasons but stays for the right one.

Congregation abets a dis-appropriation of individual subjectivity. We bring our cognitive and emotional biases into all our interactions. There is no "assumption-free" understanding, without interpreting it a priori, regardless of one's "objective" experiences.

In fact, there is no such thing as "objective experience." All experiences are subjective; only shared experiences approximate some level of objectivity. Belonging provides a unified subjectivity—a world-view based on communal assumptions, right or wrong.

Unified subjectivity means that we can only know or *unknow* together. But we can be good together, provided that we each bring goodness to the community. There is a story from the old country: A man stands by the gate of a town as he welcomes new passengers and answers their questions. One man asked what sorts of people live in this town. The guard said it depends on what kind of people lived where you are from. "If they were good people, you'll find good people in this town; if they were not, you'll find the same here." It is all about what we bring to any place, to any situation.

All religions are versions of the same truth and untruth, especially as it relates to their highly improvised rituals. The following story adapted from Carlos 8F's Zentxt, portrays the irrelevancy of seeking the truth in religious practices:

> One evening when a spiritual teacher and his disciples began their evening meditation, a cat that lived in the monastery ran amok and totally distracted them. So the teacher ordered the cat to be tied up during the evening practices. Years later, when the teacher died, the cat continued to be tied up during the meditation sessions. And when the cat died, another cat was brought to the monastery and tied up. Centuries later, learned descendants of the spiritual leader wrote many scholarly treatises about the religious significance of tying up a cat for meditation exercises.[6]

Focusing on "the untruth" of religions is missing their importance. Religions are normative institutions. They are ready-made philosophies for living and dying. Organized religion, no matter which one, is enormously attractive, contagious, and universally calming, even if it is received with deferential incredulity. Religion adds to life an enchantment, says William James "which is not rationally or logically deducible from anything else."[7]

"Homo sapiens is also Homo religiosus."[8] Like love, ambition, jealousy, and other innate impulses, our need for religion is a human instinct. "We may speak of a *religious drive,*" writes H. Bänziger "just as we speak of sexual and aggressive drives."[9]

Even our brains seem to be programmed for religion. Robert Wright says, "[if] a religious meme doesn't find a perch in individual brains, it can't spread from brain to brain and so come to characterize a whole group in the first place."[10]

The word *religion* derives from the same Latin root as the word *ligament,* which means "to bind." Religion binds us to each other. Religion is an organizational structure, a communal glue that provides a comprehensive world view. It explains everything that the human mind wonders about, whether the origin of the universe, the purpose of humanity, or the nature of an afterlife. It dictates concrete values to maintain a communal order. Religion invented God to be used for its default position, both as a potentially rewarding and punishing instrument to assure obedience to its tenets, as well as for an ideal to be emulated.

Joseph de Maistre said, "Whether religious ideas are denied or venerated is immaterial; true or false, they form the sole basis of all durable institutions."[11] Of all people, Karl Marx asserted, "Religion is the general theory of this world, its encyclopaedic compendium, its popular logic, its spiritual point of honor, its inspiration, its moral sanction, its solemn completion, its general consoling and justifying reason."[12] It frames the past, the present, and the future.

Religion, says existential philosopher William Barrett "had been a structure that encompassed man's life, providing him with a system of images and symbols by which he could express his own aspirations toward psychic wholeness. With the loss of this containing framework man became not only a dispossessed but a fragmentary being."[13]

In all religions, spirituality is considered a measure of humanity: it is the right way of being in the world: asceticism in the East, "spirit in Christianity, life in Judaism, [and] light in Islam."[14] In the West, religion promotes the cultivation of an altruistic, kind, humble, honest and virtuous self. In the East, religion interdigitates with spirituality and philosophy that emphasizes living with detachment while smiling at the world with its incomprehensible and unknowable elements. The ultimate Eastern spiritual person is an ascetic Yogi. He abstains from anger, from injuring living beings, and from appropriating the property of others. He is truthful, clean, avoids rashness, and attends to purity even in eating.

At times we confuse the message of religions with their administrative structures, or mistakenly, we seek similar engagements in the mystic edifices, or organized atrophy of churches, synagogues, mosques, temples and miss the essence of the spiritual. Idries Shah, in his book, *A Perfumed Scorpion*, tells a probably apocryphal story about a mystic shrine:

> It was customary for pilgrims to make an offering of a few yen to the custodian, a monk, who sat there all day, mostly in contemplation.
>
> A Western tourist, who nevertheless wished to have a proper respect for the properties, approached the holy place one day and , not knowing how much money to give, pulled out several thousand yen, which he offered to the monk. He was a little surprised when it was handed back to him with a smile and a shake of the head.

'I must have offered too little' he thought, and, doubling the money, he made his offering again.

The monk looked at the banknotes for a long moment. Then he shrugged and reached into a box and brought out an ancient scroll, which he presented to the visitor. And he walked away, down the road.

When translated, the mysterious document proved to be–the title–deeds to the shrine itself.[15]

An individual needs to cultivate an attitude of harmony within and without by belonging to the spiritual matrix of his/her religion and undifferentiate the self from the whole, large and small, real or imaginary.

Such outer communion means genuine engagement in an enlarging concentric dimension. Including others is a form of self-expansion. It is knitting yourself into your community. It is actually caring about all of its institutions and its people, being informed about their problems, actively participating in their solutions, as well as zestfully enjoying its celebrations. Outer communion is believing in and defending the values and principles of the community and never transgressing them. This should be easy if the personal self is aligned with the communal self and the personal philosophy within a collective framework.

Belonging takes the focusing away from yourself—a healthy decentering—and makes the congregation and its members the point of reference. A student laments to his Zen master: "I am very discouraged Master, what shall I do, what shall I do." The master replies: "Encourage others!"

Selfishness in all of its forms is an enormous breach of human etiquette, if not a serious offense. Belonging is a context in which to exercise unselfishness—true empathy; it is getting out of your own subjective framework in a radical way and gaging your interactions with others from their point of view. Simply, it is being a good person.

There may be many ways of characterizing one's goodness. Here is one from Socrates, the "Triple Filter" story:

> In ancient Greece, Socrates was reputed to hold knowledge in high esteem. One day an acquaintance met the great philosopher and said, "Do you know what I just heard about your friend?' "Hold on a minute," Socrates replied. "Before telling me anything I'd like you to pass a little test. It's called the Triple Filter Test."
>
> 'Triple filter?"
>
> "That's right," Socrates continued. "Before you talk to me about my friend, it might be a good idea to take a moment and filter what you're going to say. That's why I call it the triple filter test. The first filter is Truth. Have you made absolutely sure that what you are about to tell me is true?"
>
> "No," the man said, "Actually I just heard about it and..."
>
> "All right," said Socrates. "So you don't really know if it's true or not. Now let's try the second filter, the filter of Goodness. Is what you are about to tell me about my friend something good?"
>
> "No, on the contrary."
>
> "So," Socrates continued, "you want to tell me something bad about him, but you're not certain it's true. You may still pass the test though, because there's one filter left: the filter of Usefulness. Is what you want to tell me about my friend going to be useful to me?"
>
> "No, not really."
>
> "Well," concluded Socrates, "if what you want to tell me is neither true nor good nor even useful, why tell it to me at all?"[16]

Along the same lines, the Bible encourages honesty and discretion and discourages gossip: "Whatever you have said in the dark will be heard in the daylight. Whatever you have whispered in private rooms will be shouted front the housetops."[17]

Inner communion when coupled with our outer communion deepens the meaning of life. A meaningful individual life, therefore, needs to be framed within the meaning of the whole. It is like being a good soloist, but also being a member of an equally good orchestra.

One of the concrete demonstrations of outer-communion is sharing good fortune in a sensitive manner in widening circles of compassion. Every religion asserts that and calls on its people to be concerned about the vulnerable members of society.

The God of Israel urges compassion rather than empty prayers:

> Yes, when you make many prayers, I will not hear.
> Your hands are full of blood.
> Seek justice.
> Relieve the oppressed.
> Defend the fatherless.[18]

Almsgiving, one of the "Five Pillars" of the Islam, is commanded by the Qur'an. "Zakat [a type of charity] expresses the Islamic belief that man's stewardship of the world's resources is not for himself alone, but in the interests of society, and particularly in the care for the less fortunate members of the community."[19]

For Confucius, the paramount virtue is *ren*—a sensitive concern for others.[20]

The Bible is more specific:

> For six years you shall sow your land and gather in its increase; but the seventh year you shall let it rest and lie fallow, that the poor of your people may eat; and what they leave the animal of the field

shall eat. In the same way, you shall deal with your vineyard and with your olive grove.[21]

The following verses from the 8th century Persian poet Saadi now stand at the entrance of the headquarters of the United Nations:

> All of the sons of Adam are part of one single body,
> They are of the same essence.
> When time afflicts us with pain
> In one part of that body
> All the other parts feel it too.
> If you fail to feel the pain of others
> You do not deserve the name of man.[22]

Such generosities are most joyful if they are offered anonymously, without coveting gratitude from the receiver or exaltation from the community. Joel Kovel differentiates *egoic giving* from *soul giving. Egoic giving* is giving to gain prestige, praise, admiration, immortality; it is setting conditions for giving. In contrast, *soulful giving* is free from the burden of conditions and expectations.[23] In Sukkah (the symbol of the transience of life in Judaism), this soulful giving is called *loving kindness*. "[Loving kindness] is superior to almsgiving in the following three respects: When a man gives alms he gives merely of his possessions, whereas [loving kindness] involves giving of one's self."[24]

Thomas Moore goes one step further in advising that we should not be too protective of our belongings behind closed doors. If anything, we should keep the door ajar. "In order to have soul, we need to be taken from, and that necessary emptying requires some collusion on our part in the theft, some distraction that interferes with our intentions, some neglect in our defenses."[25]

Compassion is willingly accepting someone's counterfeit coins.

There is another form of giving that transcends our own time: intergenerational giving. In contemporary giving, the receiver may or may not know who we are; but we know the receiver. Such immediacy of the good deed has its own pleasure. But doing a good deed for the future, to an unknown receiver, generates an unusual *givers' high.* "It is more blessed to give than to receive,"[26] says the Bible. That exalted feeling is best manifested in *intergenerational generosity*, i.e., ultimate compassion. We all inherited such gifts from previous generations: parks, gardens, roads, schools, hospitals, etc. Such devotional giving become continuous generosities from one generation to another that generates communities of belonging.

In a thirteenth century Sufi tale, the old and sick Nasreddin Hoca was trying to plant an orange tree. A passerby watched and said in pity: "Dear Hoca, why on earth do you even bother to plant a tree whose fruit you'll never live long enough to eat?" Hoca replied, "That is true. But it is truer still that I have eaten plenty of fruit from the trees that others planted. "[27] No seed ever sees its flower.

In a similar vein, happiness is in the cultivation of one's garden, says Voltaire in Candide's voice.[28] But ultimate happiness comes from the cultivation of others' gardens.[29]

NOTES

1. Johann Wolfgang von Goethe, "Book II, Chapter II" in *Wilhelm Meister's Apprenticeship and Travels, Volume I,* trans. Thomas Carlyle

(New York: A.L. Burt, Publisher). (Project Gutenberg eBook #36483, 2011).

2. Ecclesiastes 4:12.

3. Proverbs 27:17.

4. EH Erikson and JM Erikson, *The Life Cycle Completed: Extended Version* (New York: Norton, 1997), 62; 79.

5. Harold Kushner, *When Bad Things Happen to Good People* (New York: Avon Books, 1981), 121–122.

6. "Ritual Cat," Zen Stories to Tell Your Neighbors, retrieved August 2, 2018. http://users.rider.edu/~suler/zenstory/ritualcat.html.

7. William James, *The Varieties of Religious Experience*, (New York: Longmans, Green, and Co. 1902), 47.

8. Karen Armstrong, *A History of God: The 4,000-Year Quest of Judaism, Christianity, and Islam* (New York: Ballantine Books, 1993), xix.

9. H. Bänziger in Viktor E. Frankl, *The Unconscious God: Psychotherapy and Theology* (New York: Simon & Schuster, 1975), 64.

10. Robert Wright, *The Evolution of God* (New York: Back Bay Books, 2009), 66.

11. Joseph de Maistre, quoted in Henri De Lubac, *The Drama of Atheist Humanism*, trans. Edith M. Riley (New York: Sheed &Ward, 1950), 45.

12. Karl Marx, "Introduction to a Contribution to the Critique of Hegel's Philosophy of Right." *Deutsch-Französische Jahrbucher, February, 1844*, Marxist Internet Archive, retrieved June 29, 2018. https://www.marxists.org/archive/marx/works/1843/critique-hpr/intro.htm.

13. William Barrett, *Irrational Man* (New York: Doubleday, 1962), 35.

14. T. Byram Karasu, *The Art of Serenity*, 223.

15. Idries Shah, *A Perfumed Scorpion* (London: The Octagon Press, 2000), 173.

16. "Testing for Gossip, #6 (Triple Filter Test)," Roger Darlington's World, last modified August 7, 2017. Retrieved June 29, 2018. http://www.rogerdarlington.me.uk./stories.html#Story50.

17. Luke 12:3.

18. Isaiah 1:15-17.

19. M. Rasjidi, "Chapter V. Islam," in *The Meaning of Life in Five Great Religions*, ed. Randolf C. Chalmers and John A. Irving (Toronto: Ryerson Press, 1965), 133.

20. Robert Wright, *The Evolution of God*, 237.

21. Exodus 23:10-11.

22. "Iranian Poetry 'Bani Adam' Inscribed on United Nations Building Entrance," 9/17/11. Retrieved July 11, 2018. http://www.zaufishan.co.uk/2011/09/iranian-poetry-bani-adam-inscribed-on.html.

23. Joel Kovel, *History and Spirit: An Inquiry into the Philosophy of Liberation* (Boston: Beacon Press, 1991), 221.

24. Sukkah 49b, in Moses H. Luzzatto, *Mesillat Yesharim*, trans. Mordecai M. Kaplan (Philadelphia: Jewish Publication Society, 2010), 201.

25. Thomas Moore, *Original Self: Living with Paradox and Authenticity* (New York: HarperCollins, 2000), 28.

26. Acts 20:35.

27. Turkish tale, in Oner Yagci, *Nasreddin Hoca Ve Fikralori* (Istanbul: Engin Yayincilik, 1994), 169.

28. Voltaire, *Candide*, trans. Lowell Blair (New York: Bantam Books, 1981), 20.

29. T. Byram Karasu, *The Art of Serenity*, 86.

Lesson Four

Marry

Mute your "I" for "we," and be a 'life witness'

This is now bone of my bones, and flesh of my flesh.[1]

Marriage is a long-term commitment between two people to share their lives. Though this is the basic template, there are many variations. Marriage is neither sex, nor love, although it has both these elements. It is definitely not the wedding. Pamela Paul, in *The Starter Marriage*, says,

> We assume that once you're wed, the rest falls into place—the beautiful home, the gourmet dinner parties attended by other witty, vivacious couples, the glorious pregnancy—with a trouble-free healthy baby. . . . The kids who always do their homework and get into prestigious schools, the fabulous family vacations . . . ultimately, home fires burning into the golden years. All you need to do is marry; the attendant rewards are waiting[2]
>
> Rarely does it happen that way.

In a 1999 article in the *New York Times*, Peter Godwin[3] writes of the American obsession with marriage, as evidenced by the enormous wedding industry. He says, "Indeed, it's no coincidence that our interest in marriage's storybook representations grows just as fast as our practical evidence of its failures." Our American "penchant" for serial marriages, he adds, "is a perfect testament to the repeated triumph of hope over experience." Dalma Heyn shares her experience that many women felt something was "very wrong" even as they were walking down the aisle. "Not with the relationship, necessarily, but in the stunning dissonance between what they were supposed to feel and what they actually felt. They had the unmistakable sense that life as they knew it was forever ending." She calls the dissonance "marriage shock." "I do" becomes "I should."[4] In *Against Love*, Laura Kipnis makes the same point about both sexes, namely that marriage is about rules and prohibitions and expectations, or as she says, "a catalogue of strictures, commands, and punishments so unending you begin to wonder why no one has yet evoked the Geneva Convention."[5]

In *Coming to Life*, therapist Leston Havens expresses a thought recognizable to many couples: "Most loving couples begin their relationship with a stern resolution to honor and respect, and yet they have hardly left the church before the slowness of one or the haste of the other, the disappointment of one expectation or the unwanted fulfillment of another, reveals the snarling beast."[6] After ecstasy, the laundry, says Zen master.

The current emphasis on planning and the money spent on some weddings overshadows the required thoughtful process of whether one should get married to a particular person or even whether one should get married. Friedan felt that marriage should be seen without the "veil of over-glorification."[7] "How well do we know the other person's inner life? More so, how well do we know our own?" Within some demographics over 50 % of marriages end up in divorce because these simple questions are not asked at the beginning. "Only by avoiding the beginning of things," says Cyril Connolly, "can we escape their endings."[8]

Even under the best circumstances, there is no guarantee that a marriage will survive. There are interacting biological, psychological, social, financial, and situational variables that may influence the outcome. All of these issues demand an emotional literacy and at least a rudimentary knowledge of and competence in marital relationships, and mastering one's own ambivalence. It is normal to remain ambivalent about being married and to whom. Objective criteria of choosing a spouse go only so far in an inter-subjective field. Furthermore, a human being is an ambivalent creature. The ultimate ambivalent being, Kierkegaard called himself a "subjective thinker." Apparently, in his native city of Copenhagen, so the story is reported by William Barrett, perhaps apocryphally, the street urchins used to run after Kierkegaard yelling "Either/or? Either/or!"[9]

Biological/anatomical differences between men and women are obvious. But not every male is male, and not every female is female. Gender is a spectrum condition. Furthermore, gender identity, that sense of maleness/femaleness, overrides biological/anatomical identity, as validated by homosexuality, asexuality, and transgender.

Sex is one of the conflict-laden subjects in marriage. Adam ate the apple; we are still having indigestion. In the early "two-strangers" phase of a marriage, dopamine levels rise in both the male and female brain and generate excitement and motivation for this novel sexual experience. As the novelty wears off over time, sex declines.

Couples differ in their hormonal states and their sexual interests. The desire hormone is testosterone, which is always present in men, and may peak anytime when stimulated—the source of their priapic preoccupation. "Of the delights of this world." says Mark Twain "man cares most for sexual intercourse. He will go to any length for it—risk fortune, character, reputation, life itself."[10]

In women, testosterone level is relatively low and fluctuates with the menstrual cycle. Testosterone in women rises only during menstruation and ovulation. Women are biologically available for sex at any time. They may be most interested in sex, however, at different times during their cycles—at ovulation, when a woman is most fertile (a kind of "pregnancy instinct"), and during menstruation ("safe pleasure instinct.")[11] If the man wants receptivity to his sexual advances he must time those advances accordingly. Other times, he may resort to inducing two other hormones in himself and in his female partner through less potent and rather indirect hormones. These are "bonding" hormones: oxytocin (more in women) and vasopressin (more in men). That means that a man must get in touch with his inner female, i.e., be affectionate, caring, comforting, listening, cuddling, romancing, attentive and patient.

While during their monthly cycle, where testosterone is higher, for women, sex is erotic, selfish, urgent and spontaneous like in men; at other times it is rather sensual, altruistic, calm, and intentional. While erotic sex hardly needs foreplay, sensual sex demands inventive foreplay. Man should neither take the foreplay as *forework* just to be gotten over nor neglect the post-coital romance and a loving presence, if he wants a repeat performance. Conditioning requires gratification.

An *un-aphrodisiac* effect of marital life is equally applicable to women and men. Monogamy diminishes not only a man's libido; it also lowers his testosterone level. Each new female contact, on the other hand, has the power to produce a new burst of sexual interest and energy. This has become known as "the Coolidge Effect," so-named after an oft-repeated (perhaps apocryphal) tale told about President Calvin Coolidge:

> The President and the first lady were given separate tours of a model farm. Coolidge's wife, upon observing an active group of chickens in the yard, noted that the rooster was being kept quite occupied. She suggested that her husband might be quite interested in her observation. When Mr. Coolidge arrived at the chicken coop, the guide promptly relayed the following message: "Your wife wanted me to point out how frequently the rooster copulated in a single day." The President deep in thought, then asked, "Same hen?" "No, Mr. President," replied the guide. "Well," said Coolidge, "tell *that* to the First Lady."[12]

The libidos of both men and women also decline within the context of a monogamous relationship. Says comedian Bill Maher, "Every marriage is *same sex* marriage. It is the same sex every night"[13] at best. Furthermore, sexuality and the sexual needs of individuals change over time naturally, with age, illnesses, stresses, or having children. Sometimes a partner will desexualize the relationship by self-neglect, excessive body exposure, or playing child or parent roles with the spouse, etc. You cannot expect romantic security while indulging in conjugal coziness.

At any stage of a marriage sexual difficulties may reflect common manifestations of marital conflicts. That is why sex therapists that exclusively focus on technical aspects of a couple's sexual conflicts tend to fail, if they do not address the couple's larger interpersonal issues. A couple comes to see a therapist. The wife complains about her husband's lack of sexual desire and poor performance. The therapist looks at him, being at least a hundred pounds overweight, suggests that before they go any further he should walk ten miles in the next ten days and then call him. The couple leaves and ten days later the therapist receives a call from the husband: 'Doc, I have done exactly what you ordered. I have walked 10 miles every day.' The therapist, very pleased with the compliance of the patient, asks: 'So how is it? Is your wife any happier?' The man puzzled says: 'How do I know, doc? I am exactly 100 miles away!'

Although it absorbs so much psychological energy and creates so many interests and conflicts, actual sex itself actually occupies a very small portion of life. For two individuals, whether heterosexual or homosexual couples, marriage is primarily about navigating the ordinariness of everyday life, in tandem. In a good marriage the exalted emotional highs are framed in a *lullness*. We need to come to terms with the limitation of marriage without looking for that illusionary perfect marriage. "Le mieux est l'ennemie du bien,"[14] says Voltaire.

Although a marriage is more than the sum of two spouses,[15] as an institution, it can only be as good as its two partners. In fact, our marriages are another manifestation of ourselves, our personality, especially our temperament. Wherever we go we'll be taking ourselves there, whether to a marriage, to a job, or to a friendship. Á la Odysseus, our psychological DNA-based story stops, but never ends.

The word "temperament" is related to the word "temper," the hardness imparted to a metal. Its intractable quality was expressed in Lewis Carroll's *Through the Looking Glass*, when the Red Queen meanly interrogated Alice about her inability to do division, addition, and subtraction. Making sure that she fails, she demands of Alice to try another subtraction sum.

> "Take a bone from a dog: what remains?" Alice considered. "The bone wouldn't remain, of course, if I took it—and the dog wouldn't remain: it would come to bite me—and I'm sure I shouldn't remain!" "Then you think nothing would remain?' said the red Queen. "I think that's the answer." "Wrong as usual," said the Red Queen—"the dog's temper would remain."[16]

Some couples tune into different frequencies; others are uncommonly in tune with each other. Two best soloists do not necessarily make a great duo, unless they synchronize; and that synchronization takes considerable practice. This requires couples listening to each other with full presence. Alice Walker, in an interview, reportedly described how a woman in her novel *The Temple of My Familiar* falls in love with a particular man because she sees in him "a giant ear." Our conversations tend to be simultaneous monologues. We need to listen to each other with every part of our bodies, like Helen Keller. In *The Story of My Life*, she writes, "I cannot make notes during lectures because my hands are very busy listening."[17]

"There is no absolute reality in marital conflict, only two subjective realities,"[18] according to marital therapists John M. Gottman and Nan Silver. That is partly why people seek out couples' therapists: maieutic listeners—dialogue in the form of Socratic midwifery—with an offer of an unconscious hand, whenever needed.

Besides attentive listening with introspection, as in all joint efforts, you also have to bring a good mood and a softened affect to the marriage, because emotions are contagious and unconsciously infecting. You should cultivate your independent interests as well as your joint interests. Let go of each other in order to keep each other. Sogyal Rinpoche tells a charming vignette:

> Pick up a coin. Hold it tightly clutched in your fist and extend your arm with the palm of your hand facing the ground. Now if you let go or relax your grip, you will lose what you are clinging onto. But there is another possibility: With your arm still outstretched, turn your hand over so that it faces the sky. Release your hand and the coin still rests on your open palm. You let go. And the coin is still yours, even with all this space around it.[19]

We can only be together by being separate. Co-independent partners know how to be alone in each other's presence. Love one another, but make not a bondage of love… Fill each other's cup, but don't drink from the same cup. . . Stand together yet not too near to each other; For the pillars of the temple stand apart. And the oak tree and the cypress tree grow not in each other's shadow.[20]

Do not play maestro, teacher, therapist, or any other kind of caretaker role in the marriage: *spousehood* is plenty enough. When one member of the pair assumes a role of caretaker, pity or self-pity also enters the picture, undoing the sexual desire. So it was in the story of King David:

> "Now King David was old and stricken in years; and they covered him with clothes, but he got no heat. Wherefore his servants said unto him, Let there be sought for my lord the king a young virgin: and let her stand before the king, and let her cherish him, and let her lie in thy bosom, that my lord the king may get heat. So they sought a fair damsel throughout all the coasts of Israel, and found Abishag

> a Shunammite, and brought her to the king. And the damsel was very fair, and cherished the king, and ministered to him: but the king knew her not."[21]

The development of intimacy in marriage requires spouses to survive many adversities, challenges, failings and successes, develop their own emotional vocabulary and weave each other into a sort of psychological hermaphroditism. The innate capacities to love develop only when one is loved by someone in those *tabula rasa* years. The lack of being loved warps the childhood nucleus, handicapping the person in loving others. Such deprived people have to learn how to love, by being loved by contemporary empathetic figures, i.e. spouses, if lucky. Emotionally miserly or emotionally incontinent spouses are destabilizing, frequently with syndromal manifestations. Sometimes symptoms are ways of dealing with spouses. The recipient spouse who experiences such pathology must not retreat to defensive emotional hibernation but fight for the marriage; otherwise a personal inner deadness sets in.

Fights are as important in forming emotional intimacy as love. In Noël Coward's play, *Private Lives*,[22] Amanda asks Elyot whether they will always want to bicker and fight, "No, that desire will fade, with our passion," says Elyot. Most likely Coward's couple has contentious or *de-familiarizing* arguments—foreplay for their passion, rather than real fights. If the couple does not establish an emotional intimacy as well, quarrels create passion-fueled further alienation and a sense of aloneness.

Real combats are related to too much truth and lies. Some people have love affairs; others are just sexually promiscuous. Some people seek relationships with many others—a sort of *platonic promiscuity*, a term of Edward Hoagland, in his essay

Strange Perfume.[23] Some others are too obsessed with parrhesia (unchecked frankness) to the detriment of their relationship. A truth, says William Blake, "with bad intent beats all the lies you can invent."[24]

Some truths are simply exploitative. Kierkegaard thought of "truth-as-self-coincidence:" Writes Daniel Watts, "...objective and subjective truth are not, for Kierkegaard, different *kinds* of truth but, rather, different ways in which truth manifests itself as a standard of success across different contexts of inquiry."[25] Truth is subjective—"'the self-identity' of thought and being," and within this philosophy, Kierkegaard considered that pure objectivity is not possible to achieve—because we can never view the truth dispassionately. One aspect of "truth-as-self-coincidence" is that it "admits of degrees," says Watts. We may be accused of bad motives and bad feelings, of jealousy, betrayal, or ungratefulness.

Not just in marriage, but in life, neither seeking the truth, nor delivering it, may be salutary or desirable, without requiring editing ears. Such lack of appreciation for the truth was recorded in 1 Kings 22:1–19 at the time of King Zedekiah:

> King Ahab of Israel and King Jehoshaphat of Judah were dressed in royal robes and seated on thrones. . . All of the prophets were prophesying in front of them. Zedekiah, son of Chenaanah, made iron horns, and spoke: "This is what the Lord says—with these horns you will push the Arameans to their destruction." All of the other prophets made the same prophecy. They said, "Attack Ramoth in Gilead, and you will win. The Lord will hand it over to you."
>
> Then Micaiah, a renegade prophet, was summoned for his prophecy. The messenger who went to find Micaiah told him:

'The Prophets have all told the King the same good message. Make your message agree with their message. Say something good." To this order, Micaiah answered, "I solemnly swear, as the Lord lives, I will tell him whatever my God says to me." When he came to the King and was asked, "Micaiah, should we go to war against Ramoth in Gilead or not?" Micaiah replied, "Attack, and you will win. They will be handed over to you." The King then asked him, "How many times must I make you take an oath in the Lord's name to tell me nothing but the truth?" At this Micaiah responded, "I saw Israel's troops scattered in the hills, like sheep without a shepherd." At this, the King of Israel turned to Jehoshaphat, "Didn't I tell you he wouldn't prophesy anything good about me?"

Every lie is a sort of confession. Undoing lies told "with good intent" could have bad consequences, especially if the truth is not delivered in a single installment. Otherwise gradual revelation generates doubt, in which, says Baltasar Gracián, "the liar suffers twice; he neither believes, nor is believed."[26] The major damage of falsehoods, however, is the disruption of intimacy between two people—even if the lie is never detected. This is because the liar can no longer be totally genuine, sincere, unguarded, and authentic in that relationship. Duplicity and intimacy are mutually exclusive, whether the nature of the transgression is in bad or in good faith. "Make a hair's difference and Heaven and earth are set apart," rewording Hsin Hsin Ming.

Couples can lie, tell the truth, play, laugh, cry and also fight, without the melodrama of right or wrong, but should never draw emotional blood from each other. Men and women are infinitely ingenious in their ability to find new ways of being unhappy together.[27] On the other hand, sedated peace does not necessarily make a better marriage. All sunshine makes a desert, says the Arabian proverb. Even Billy Graham's wife was not immune from having rage against her husband. When asked whether she ever thought of divorcing him, she said, "Divorce? No. Murder? Yes"[28] and laughed.

Everyone brings his or her own fire to hell, but there is one common source of fire that some couples share: mutual objectification. Such fights have the cadence of *psychological embalmment or cannibalism*. A man and woman in an intimate relationship, especially in a marriage, "treat one another with cruelty that they would never consider directing toward anyone who meant less to them."[29]

Couples have to remain truthful but not vicious, hard but not injurious, passionate but compassionate, and always highly tuned into linguistic feelings. There can be no wallowing in the warmth of righteousness, no stripping each other psychologically bare and leaving the other utterly vulnerable. The purpose of fighting is not to win (it is vulgar to win always) or to hurt another but to establish even stronger bonds.

Fights should never attempt to mute or lower another person's self-esteem or make the other person feel guilty or use him/her as a dumping ground for one's own personal frustrations unrelated to the marriage. What is worse than the emotional callousness of a bad fight is emotional absence—a barbed aloofness—of the spouse or anyone else for that matter. The Bible puts it poetically: "We played the flute for you, and you didn't dance. We mourned for you, and you didn't lament."[30]

Spouses also tend to diagnose each other, as a form of attack, calling the other a malignant narcissist, a demented psychotic, infantile, or more commonly "not normal." You should know that none of us is the point of reference for normality; we should not expect another to be our psychological clone. You should accept each other as is; in fact, you should celebrate your differences, at least in the quiet togetherness of married hours. Aggressions toward spouses may be related to the aggressor's lack of interest in finding the inner core of his/her spouse or reflecting plain ignorance. Once, when I raised that possibility in a counseling session, a husband replied: 'I don't know, and I don't care.'

We can all avoid so much pain if we get to know each other. Aristotle could have avoided the mistake of thinking that women have fewer teeth than men by the simple device of asking Mrs. Aristotle to open her mouth.[31] Equally, the great question, says Freud "which I have not been able to answer, despite my thirty years of research into the feminine soul, is "What does a woman want?"[32] Too bad, he could have asked his wife. What does a woman want? Sarah Ban Breathnach's in *Simple Abundance*, answers that complex question of Freud with a deceptively simple answer: "A nap, Dr. Freud, a nap."[33]

You can grow and mature better within the context of love. "Thus wondrously within your eyes, I saw myself unfold,"[34] says Friedrich Hebbel. In marriages as well as in other situations, there is a cumulative effect of human relationships, good and bad; bad ones nurse ill-defined resentments, good ones promote growth. Psychoanalyst Henry Dicks[35] suggests that even infidelity may be a necessary crisis in the growth process of a couple. That may be so, provided that other spouses remain within the boundaries of fair reciprocity and maintain what Ivan Boszormenyi-Nagy and Barbara R. Krasner call some "residual trust."[36] These authors believe loss of trustworthiness or merit is rarely absolute. They accept that each relationship contains an invisible slate or "ledger of give-and-take," what Peter Kramer calls a "trust fund"[37]: "Strong balance sheets make stable marriages. But if one partner continually overdraws the account, the other will feel justified in retaliating or leaving."

Daily conflicts in marriages are predictably generic and have little to do with severe transgression as much as living with another person. This is due in part because there are really two marriages in every marital union: the husband's and the wife's. What makes heterosexual marriage difficult is the fact that it is between a man and a woman. In many ways they are different species. They even have their own *genderlects* and emotional dialectics, operating within their own biologically-designed script. For example, most men are jealous but the intensity of jealousy in women is total. Every woman by nature seems to exclude all other women, including her mother-in-law.

Most married women complain of not having enough linguistic intercourse with their spouses. For them, the content is unimportant. Most men's conversations are specific and content-dependent, with no tolerance for redundancies. "Get to the point" regularly says a man to his wife. In communicative intimacy the shortest distance between two points is not a direct line. Trouble talk is the ritual lament of women, and men have a desire (and inability) to fix it: men's digital "report talk" and women's verbal grooming "rapport talk" are the source of generic conflicts between the discordant minds of men and women. They edit each other constantly. Men and women steadily perform an "oral form of back-seat driving"[38] on each other, says a character in De Vries's *Reuben, Reuben.* Focusing on such unchangeable gender differences fuels spouses' normal ambivalences about the other.

Children compound marital conflicts but seeds of these discords are sown long before the first baby arrives.[39] They just compound those existing conflicts: young ones by attachment and triangulating, as the mother shifts her attention to the children, her biological extensions; adolescents by distancing and negating, as a father shifts his attention to adolescents, his social/professional extensions.

Adolescents eventually disobey, to negate both parents, sometimes harshly—an inevitable *parentectomy*—once they bite the primordial apple—sex. God told Adam about the apple, and since He is omnipotent, He "…must have known very well that man was going to eat the forbidden fruit,"[40] says Joseph Campbell, in his book *The Power of Myth*, a conversation between him and journalist Bill Moyers. "But it was by doing that," continues Campbell, "that man became the initiator of his own life. Life really began with that act of disobedience." Parents shouldn't react with disapproval to their children's attempts for independence; if anything, they should facilitate it because it is not easy for adolescents to leave the "cocoon." Birds gently push their babies from the nest, in spite of their hesitations and even heart-wrenching protestations. In *Soul Mates*, Thomas Moore discusses that Adam and Eve were the first to be expelled from Paradise, and according to some tradition, their Fall was even considered *felix culpa*, a "fortunate error."[41] Through their errors, mistakes, bad judgments, conflicts, and emotional battles, parents invariably set the stage for children—postadolescence—to leave home.

Having children may certainly enrich the lives of a couple, but also may deprive them from the exclusive emotional and sexual attention of the partner. Various neurotic scenarios emerge as the family enlarges. At times, parents will join children to compound emerging conflicts between them. According to Susan Maushart, when children reach adolescence, spouses tend to like each other less.[42] These are the times when a marriage may need steady ear-to-ear resuscitations.

Parents can turn siblings against each other in spite of their love by favoring one over another. The biblical children Cain and Abel were a case in point. In Genesis 4:1-8, so the narrative goes, these two sons of Adam brought offerings to the Lord: Cain brought some crops, as he was a farmer, and Abel, some choice parts of the first-born animals from his flock, as he was a shepherd. When the Lord approved of Abel and his offering and didn't approve of Cain's contribution, Cain became very angry, and later when they were in the fields together, Cain killed Abel. It wasn't rejection of his gift, nor even rejection of himself that converted Cain's anger into murder, but God's approval of his brother Abel.[43]

As spouses age, they experience different dilemmas. Aging intensifies the personal traits of a person, as well as his/her expectations in and frustration from the marriage. Loneliness is one of the unspoken disappointments in marriages; paradoxically, the fear of being alone in life is one reason why people are interested in marriage. Of course, all depends on who you are and whom you marry. Chekhov wrote, "If you are afraid of loneliness, don't marry."[44] "Loneliness" is a word everyone thinks he understands, says Helen Deutsch. "I have come to my own precise definition: that person is lonely who has no one for whom he or she is Number One."[45] This is a very high bar—an unrealistic expectation from without. An individual who is not personally fulfilled from within cannot expect a marriage to repair that emptiness. The commonly found solution for such chronic frustration in marriage, i.e., divorce, does not end this personal unhappiness; it only compounds it. That may be one of the reasons why "I hate divorce," says the Lord.[46]

A divorce becomes legitimate when one receives contempt, disgust, physical or psychological abuse, humiliation or neglect from the spouse. In such circumstances, an emotional divorce has already occurred, long before the actual divorce. Some couples inhabit a "marital ghetto," which Michael Vincent Miller defines as "the human equivalent of a balanced aquarium, where the fish and plants manage to live off each other's waste products."[47] This degree of negativity in marriage, if allowed to run rampant, is lethal to the people involved. John M. Gottman and Nan Silver highlight "criticism," "contempt," "defensiveness," and "stonewalling" as the "Four Horsemen of the Apocalypse."[48] Cynthia Heimel, in "Beware of Mr. Right," wonders why we are not even telling, if not shouting, the awful truth of marriage: "How do marriage counselors sleep at night, knowing all they know about marriage and not screaming it to the world?"[49]

Judith Viorst, in *Suddenly Sixty and Other Shocks of Later Life,*[50] brings a sense of humor to such a pessimistic view of marriages:

A Very, Very Brief History of Marriage

1963 Niagara
1999 Viagra

That may apply to the sexual marital life but not necessarily to the emotional marital life. In the same vein, Ehrenreich contrasts love with marriage: "Love is something wild and crazy, while marriage is sober and sane."[51]

Marriage has been compared to a kind of cage; inside there are birds trying to get out, as they look at freely flying birds; meanwhile birds outside are trying to get in as they see the crumbs within. In spite of all its shortcomings, marriage is better than being alone. Genesis 2:18 says: "It is not good for the man to be alone." There are also a number of citations in the Bible against marriage. Nevertheless, research shows that a good marriage is good for both sexes, and even may result in better physical health for each.

The need to be married manifests differently in men and women. Obviously generalization notwithstanding, a women's *inner girl*, a source of her neurosis of abandonment, needs a strong man. Colette Dowling calls this yearning a *Cinderella Complex*: "the deep wish to be taken care of."[52]

The *inner boy* of men craves a maternal wife, whenever he is not sexually preoccupied. M.V. Miller tells the following story:

> First God made Adam, but Adam complained that he was lonely. So God put him to sleep and made Eve from Adam's rib. When Adam awoke, he beheld a gorgeous female standing before him. Yet, he still looked miserable, so God appeared and asked him: "What is bothering you now, Adam? Look at the beautiful wife I made for you!" Adam replies, "Yes, but first I need a mother."[53]

A marriage based on excessive neediness or dependency festers in domestic pity, synthetic love, and fake contentment. Real contentment comes from mutual confirmation, psychological loyalty, and idealization of the partner (so-called *overshooting*), deserved or not. In "A Leap of Faith?"[54] and "The (Mental) Ties That Bind,"[55] researchers Sandra L. Murray and John G. Holmes found that couples' abilities to idealize their partners—the relationship illusion—predicted greater satisfaction and less conflict in marriage. Partners create stories they tell themselves and the world about each other whereby they tend to exaggerate the good qualities and minimize (or even perhaps, deny) the bad qualities of their partners. This may not always be possible. Marriage like life itself should be viewed as "full of undershootings as well as overshootings but always progressing toward a fated destination."[56]

While holding on tightly to his wife Jacqueline's hand, Picasso's deathbed statement to his confirmed bachelor physician was "you are wrong not to marry, it is useful."[57] Marriage is more than useful. A good marriage is at its best when two equals become life witnesses to each other in co-independent, *un-counterfeitable* love and friendship. Love takes "I ness" away. Iconic humorist Mark Twain was quite serious about marriage and takes a long view:

> Love seems the swiftest, but it is the slowest of all growths. No man or woman really knows what perfect love is until they have been married a quarter of a century.[58]
>
> As we get older, we begin to appreciate the harmony and preciousness of being cherished by one person with whom we have shared life, after many others have more or less deserted us. This is similar to the last movement of Haydn's 1772 Symphony No. 45, in f-sharp Minor, *Farewell.* Apparently, so the anecdote goes, Haydn wrote in this manner as requested by his musicians, who were performing out of town and expressed to him their wish to return home as soon as possible to their spouses and families. Describes music critic Michael Steinberg, "The music resumes, and one by one, instruments play farewell solos and leave . . . .The survivors play the gently pathos-filled slow music again. The cello leaves, then all the violins, but two, then the viola." The two violins remain to play a haunting melody "leaving us somewhere between tears and a smile."

Similarly, in the final movement of a successful marriage, life together continues after children, grandchildren, friends, colleagues leave, one by one, to return to their own homes. Husband and wife remain alone as life-witnesses to each other, as the two violins faithfully continue to play a melody full of tears and smiles.[59]

NOTES

1. Genesis 2:23.
2. Pamela Paul, *The Starter Marriage and the Future of Matrimony* (New York: Random House, 2002), 42–43.
3. Peter Godwin, "The Way We Live Now: July 25, 1999; Happily Ever After," *New York Times*, July 25, 1999, Sunday Magazine Desk, Section 6, 13.
4. Dalma Heyn, *Marriage Shock: The Transformation of Women into Wives* (New York: Random House, 1997), 88, 140.
5. Laura Kipnis, *Against Love: A Polemic* (New York: Pantheon, 2003), 83–84.
6. Leston Havens, *Coming to Life* (Cambridge: Harvard University Press, 1993), 97.
7. Betty Friedan, *The Feminine Mystique* with an Introduction by Anna Quindlen (New York: Norton, 2001), 342.
8. Cyril Connolly, *The Unquiet Grave: A Word Cycle by Palinarus* Revised Edition with an Introduction by Cyril Connolly (Read Books Ltd., 2013), 25. Google Play Books Edition.
9. William Barrett, *Irrational Man*, 152.
10. Mark Twain, *Mark Twain's Notebook in American Artists Edition of the Complete Works of Mark Twain* (New York: Harper and Brothers, 1935), 397.
11. Kalman Glantz and John K. Pearce, *Exiles from Eden: Psychotherapy from an Evolutionary Perspective* (New York: Norton, 1990), 105–106.

12. Glenn Wilson, *The Coolidge Effect: An Evolutionary Account of Human Sexuality*, (New York: William Morrow, 1982), 64–65.

13. Bill Maher, *Real Time with Bill Maher*. HBO, February 27, 2004. Television program.

14. Voltaire (Francois-Marie Arouet), *La Bégueule Edition augmentée* (Paris: Arvensa Éditions, 2014), E book EPUB # 9782368410035.

15. Stephen Nock, "The Problem with Marriage," *Society* 36 (5) (1999): 20–27.

16. Lewis Carroll, *Alice's Adventures in Wonderland and Through the Looking-Glass* With introductions by Will Self and Zadie Smith (New York: Bloomsbury, 2003), 357.

17. Helen Keller, *The Story of My Life* With an Introduction by Jim Knipfel (New York: Penguin Putnam, 1988), 74.

18. John M. Gottman and Nan Silver, *Seven Principles for Making Marriage Work* (New York: Three Rivers Press, 1999), 150.

19. Sogyal Rinpoche, *The Tibetan Book of Living and Dying*, ed. Patrick Gaffney and Andrew Harvey, 1991 reprint (New York: HarperCollins, 1994), 34.

20. Khalil Gibran, *The Prophet* (Oxford: Benedictine Classics, 2013), 8.

21. 1 Kings 1:1–4.

22. Noël Coward, *Private Lives: An Intimate Comedy* (New York: Samuel French, Inc., 1975), 33.

23. Edward Hoagland, "Strange Perfume," in *Here Lies My Heart: Essays on Why We Marry, Why We Don't and What We Find There*, Foreword by Amy Bloom, ed. Deborah Chasman and Catherine Jhee (Boston: Beacon Press, 1999), 74–96.

24. William Blake, *The Complete Poetry and Prose of William Blake*, ed. David V. Erdman (New York: Anchor Books, 1988), 491.

25. Daniel Watts, "Kierkegaard on Truth: One or Many?" *Mind* 127(505) (2018):197–223.

26. Baltasar Gracian, *The Art of Worldly Wisdom: A Pocket Oracle* trans. Christopher Maurer (New York: Doubleday, 1992), 87.

27. Lawrence S. Kubie, "Psychoanalysis and Marriage: Practical and Theoretical Issues," in *Neurotic Interaction in Marriage*, ed. Victor W. Eisenstein (New York: Basic Books, 1956), 10–43.

28. Stephen G. Scholle, Billy Graham Evangelistic Association, email to author, October 13, 2003.

29. Michael V Miller, *Intimate Terrorism: The Crisis of Love in an Age of Disillusion* (New York: Norton, 1995), 70.

30. Matthew 11:17.

31. Bertrand Russell, "An Outline of Intellectual Rubbish: A Hilarious Catalogue of Organized and Individual Stupidity," in *The Basic Writings of Bertrand Russell, 1903–1959*, ed. Lester E. Dennon (New York: A Clarion Book, Simon & Schuster, 1967), 94.

32. Ernest Jones, *Sigmund, Life and Work. Vol. 2, Years of Maturity, 1901–1919* (London: Hogarth Press, 1967), 468.

33. Sarah Ban Breathnach, *Simple Abundance: A Daybook of Comfort and Joy* (Sydney: Hodder Headline Australia, 2002), November 27.

34. Christian Friedrich Hebbel, "Tändelei," in *Sämtliche Werke, Bande II* (Emil Vollmer Verlag, Essen (no year given.), 74.

35. Henry Dicks, *Marital Tensions: Clinical Studies towards a Psychological Theory of Interaction* (New York: Basic Books, 1967), 168.

36. Ivan Boszormenyi-Nagy and Barbara R. Krasner, *Between Give and Take: A Clinical Guide to Contextual Therapy* (New York: Brunnel/Mazel, 1986), 88–89.

37. Peter Kramer, *Should You Leave?* (New York: Penguin, 1999), 55, 251.

38. Peter De Vries, *Reuben, Reuben* (New York: Little, Brown, 1964), 101–102.

39. Caroline Pape Cowan and Philip A. Cowan, *When Partners Become Parents: The Big Life Change for Couples* (New York: HarperCollins, 1992), x.

40. Joseph Campbell and Bill Moyers, *The Power of Myth*, ed. Betty Sue Flowers (New York: Doubleday, 1988), 51.

41. Thomas Moore, *Soulmates: Honoring the Mysteries of Love and Relationship* (New York: Harper-Collins, 1994), 79.

42. Susan Maushart, *Wifework: What Marriage Really Means for Women* (New York: Bloomsbury, 2001), 123.

43. Sylvia R. Karasu and T. Byram Karasu, *The Art of Marriage Maintenance*, 140.

44. Chekhov, as quoted in W. H. Auden and Louis Kronenberger, *Aphorisms* (New York, Dorset Press, 1981), 193.

45. Helene Deutsch, *Confrontations with Myself* (New York: W.W. Norton and Co, 1973), 14.

46. Malachi 2:16.

47. Michael Vincent Miller, *Intimate Terrorism: The Crisis of Love in an Age of Disillusion*, 87.

48. John M.Gottman and Nan Silver, *The Seven Principles for Making Marriage Work* (New York: Crown, 1999), 27–34.

49. Cynthia Heimel, "Beware of Mr. Right," in *Here Lies My Heart: Essays on Why We Marry, Why We Don't, and What We Find There*, 17–21.

50. Judith Viorst, "A Very, Very Brief History of Marriage," in *Suddenly Sixty and Other Shocks of Life* (New York: Simon & Schuster, 2000), 38–39.

51. Barbara Ehrenreich, "Why It Might Be Worth It (to Have an Affair)," in *Here Lies My Heart: Essays on Why We Marry, Why We Don't, and What We Find There*, 6–8.

52. Colette Dowling, *The Cinderella Complex: Women's Hidden Fear of Independence* (New York: Summit Books, 1981), 16.

53. Michael Vincent Miller, *Intimate Terrorism: The Crisis of Love in an Age of Disillusion*, 115.

54. Sandra L. Murray and John G. Holmes, "A Leap of Faith? Positive Illusions in Romantic Relationships," *Personality and Social Psychology Bulletin* 23 (6) (June 1997): 586–604.

55. Sandra L. Murray and John G. Holmes, "The (Mental) Ties That Bind: Cognitive Structures That Predict Relationship Resilience," *Journal of Personality and Social Psychology* 77 (6) (1999): 1228–44.

56. Sylvia R. Karasu and T. Byram Karasu, *The Art of Marriage Maintenance*, 222.

57. Pablo Picasso in Patrick O'Brian, *Picasso: A Biography* (New York: W. W. Norton and Co., 1976), 479.

58. Mark Twain, *Mark Twain's Notebook in American Artists Edition of the Complete Works of Mark Twain* (New York: Harper and Brothers, 1935), 235.

59. Sylvia R. Karasu and T. Byram Karasu, *The Art of Marriage Maintenance*, 222–223.

Lesson Five

De-Stress

Live a long and healthy life, and be grateful

> Shifting from "doing" to "being" creates your Zen cave—your sanctuary.

Stress is related to feeling a sense of impotence—a psychological paralysis. We can reach such impasses at work, in marriage, in health (of self or loved ones) and among many other situations. Even trivial deadlocks, real or imagined, can bring about a sense, albeit transient, of powerlessness. In fact, most of our stresses are self-induced. For some people nothing is written, unless they write it themselves. Following an accident at the picnic where his son was injured, a man bragged to his friend about his foresight in saving the day. "Thank God," he said. "I took a mule with us on the picnic, because when the boy was injured, I used the mule to carry him back." The friend asked: How did the boy get injured? The man said, "The mule kicked him!"

There is no agreed upon definition of stress, partly because stress is another spectrum condition. Although there are objective gradations and causes, it is a subjective state. For example, post-traumatic syndrome doesn't occur in every soldier on the front line. Each individual has his/her own level of tolerance for events generating physical or mental tensions. These events don't have to be negative to engender stress; positive events also can induce a surge of stress caused by neurotransmitters i.e. noradrenaline and stress hormones, e.g. cortisol in the body. A promotion, for example, as welcome news as possible, can temporarily generate enough anxiety and sleep disturbances to cause a rise of blood pressure and other somatic symptoms.

Stress hormones and neurotransmitters are on autopilot and controlled by the visceral brain (the old brain) that we share with other mammals. The hypothalamic, pituitary, adrenal axis is responsible for releasing cortisol; the sympathetic nervous system is responsible for stimulating the adrenal medulla to release adrenaline. When an external danger is sensed, the visceral brain automatically sets a person into a fight or flee mode. Such survival mechanisms are rarely useful in modern life; commonly there is no one to fight or no place to flee. When not neutralized, the excessive release of noradrenaline and cortisol floods the body and results in various physical and psychological symptoms. Stress symptoms vary; they depend on the person's genetic make-up and individual predisposition: weight losses or gains, muscle spasms, high blood pressure, allergic symptoms, hair loss, chronic colds, gastrointestinal, and cardiovascular symptoms. Many of these symptoms are somatic memories.

In contrast to other animals, we also generate internal dangers through our cortical brains. Feelings such as shame and guilt, anticipatory fears, regrets, hypochondriacal preoccupations, obsessions over trivial issues and even vague sentiments of nameless wrongs are equally powerful in generating stress symptoms. There is a close connection between the cortical and visceral brain, intertwining the psychological and biological components of the brain. When we perceive psychological stress, the old brain reacts in a similar fashion as if an external danger is at play and pours the noradrenaline and cortisol into the body.

If a stressful situation is a familiar one and does not present a threat to the homeostasis of the somatic system, it will be processed primarily by the limbic and forebrain circuit—a sort of cognitive process without many physiological and hormonal reactions. But an unfamiliar stress is always treated with physiological and hormonal responses. Then, the cortical brain also joins for appraisal of the threat, and assesses its level of controllability and social importance.

Repeated stresses induce an atrophy of the apical dendrites of the pyramidal neurons in the hippocampus, down-regulate responses to acute stresses, while suppressing our immunity and depriving a person of possible adaptive options. Stress inhibits our immunological system and thus makes all organs vulnerable to attacks from viruses, bacteria, and cancer cells. Physiological reactions to chronic stress (i.e. the surging of neurotransmitters and hormones) may cause physical trauma to the body and lower the body's resistance to illnesses. In the stressed person, viruses, which are often similar to ordinary human cells, easily settle in the body. Bacteria and their toxins weaken the cellular control mechanisms. With any kind of stress, an immunological system already under siege becomes even less effective. That is why older people tend to die often from a seemingly minor infection.

Psychological traumas are either historical and/or contemporary, both kicking up the dust from still earlier experiences. As physicist Carlo Rovelli writes in his book *The Order of Time*,[1] the past always "leaves traces of itself in the present." Each stage of development has laid its sediment, and later disturbances eject material from the strata. Furthermore, the responses of other people important to the one who has been traumatized may exacerbate the extent of the traumatization. Psychological traumas are conducive to generating anxiety, dysphoria, and pervasive fatigue, if not serious psychiatric disorders. The treatment of psychological traumas is still experimental. Although intensely reliving those experiences may have short-term value, after such "an awareness of awareness" period, we are better off not "re-imprinting" them, though some people need to remember and some need to forget. At times, there are no objective realities to our subjective experiences; they may, in fact, be simply inherited memories. Regardless, our own story often becomes self-legitimizing and perpetuates ongoing editions as the past is created at every instant. You need to learn from the past, not to repeat it, literally or psychologically.

Repeated stresses do not allow homeostasis to return in a timely fashion. It takes about 90 minutes for our metabolism to return to its baseline. Chronic stress down-regulates corticotropin-releasing hormone, but increases arginine vasopressor that flattens, if not erases our circadian rhythms, and creates serious health problems: sleep disturbances, eating disorders, very high blood pressure, and decrease of sperm or egg counts. Spermatogenesis, incidentally, is a very good measure of wellness in men.

Chronic traumatic experiences may eventually overwhelm a person and produce concomitant changes in his/her psychological and physiological state. The hippocampus may shrink and result in impairment of thoughts and affects, and, in fact, even alter our self-concept and personality. Neuroscientists now believe that such neurological vulnerability may even create genetic alterations.

Severe traumas, especially those that are chronic (lasting a long time), rather than being acute discrete events, leave their imprints on our psyches, commonly as emotional numbness and confusion. Viktor Frankl, in an extreme example, has described his and fellow inmates' experiences after being saved and liberated from a concentration camp:

> We came to meadows full of flowers. We saw and realized that they were there, but we had no feelings about them. The first spark of joy came when we saw a rooster with a tail of multicolored feathers. But it remained only a spark; we did not yet belong to this world. In the evening when we all met again in our hut, one said secretly to the other, "Tell me, were you pleased today?" And the other replied, feeling ashamed as he did not know that we all felt similarly, "Truthfully, no!" We had literally lost the ability to feel pleased and had to relearn it slowly.[2]

Frankl likens this liberation numbness to deep-sea divers in a decompression chamber, a kind of psychological counterpart of the bends. Long-lasting chronic traumas accumulatively generate analogous stresses that require decompression chambers.

There is another stress, a silent stress that is less recognized: chronic mental fatigue. Commonly there are no identifiable physical or psychological traumas. Betty Friedan[3] talks about good, bad, and worst fatigues. *Good fatigue* is an overload of the brain, but the work is within its domain. This stress is not distress; it is "eustress"—a pleasant stress. The brain can recover fast enough with some downtime. It is like *rallentando* in music, a gradual slackening of tempo, a winding down. *Good fatigue* is preventable by integrating rest into your work schedule. Work and rest are like different points on life's wave as they balance each other, says Alex Soojung-Kim Pang.[4]

Bad fatigue occurs if the brain is forced to perform a task that is not within its natural proclivities. For example, this may occur when right brain-lateralized people face complicated mathematical challenges. As a result, there is a sense of defeat and a feeling of "stupidity" that compounds the stress of the task. No amount of downtime activities can help that person resume the task successfully. The Bible urges simplicity, and common sense: "See that all these things are done in wisdom and order; for it is not requisite that a man should run faster than he has strength."[5]

The worst fatigue is *numbing fatigue*, i.e. when one is being strapped to repetitious, unrewarding mindless activities that put the brain in a state of "cruise control" and the person into boredom, which manifests in the form of anxiety and a tedium of existence. *Bad fatigue* is dealt with by changing the field and finding a job suitable for that brain. Numbing fatigue requires changing the context of our social/economic conditions. Both bad and numbing fatigue transmit the stress to others, including family members, colleagues, proliferating their impacts.

These interconnections between the visceral and cortical brain do not always lead to stress; in fact, they can be extremely useful as well. The visceral brain controls all autonomous functions such as sleep, the cardiovascular, pulmonary and gastrointestinal systems, sex and pregnancy-related physiological activities and the immunological system. In short, the old brain is responsible for our physical homeostasis. In favorable times, it can also produce those so-called "feel-good hormones," such as oxytocin, estradiol, testosterone, and so-called "feel-good" neurotransmitters such as serotonin and endorphins, and excitement-generating dopamine. They are responsible for our general feeling of psychological wellness. True health is never felt.

Subjected to the same stress, potentially we all react differently. The plasticity of our neuro-endocrinological system contributes significantly to our ability to adapt to a life-course trajectory and the shifting landscape of stress across time. Each individual has his/her own physical and psychological DNAs, history, biorhythms, i.e., the principle *authorythmia*, and even variations of neuroses. Ultimately, the degree of our internal disorganization determines the outcome. No matter how subtle, there are infinite varieties of minds and brains. Our mind/brain—software/hardware structures—determine how we understand and process external and internal stimuli. The mind is the qualitative factor in computer terminology, i.e. the software system; it functions in relation to internal and external reference points and thus is always shifting. Tibetan masters have compared mind (*sem*) to a candle flame, vulnerable to all the winds of circumstance, in an open doorway. As such, seen from a single stance, *sem* is "irregularly flickering and unstable."[6] There is another noteworthy term in Buddhism, writes Herbert Benson, "that depicts this mental chaos, papañca. It means 'monkey mind.'"[7] "Its analogy is to monkeys who jump repeatedly from one tree limb to another. Comparatively, the human mind can leap from thought to thought, with no interruption. When this 'monkey mind' phenomenon occurs, there is usually excessive brain activity that overloads the brain."[8] The mind is a subjective instrument, whose functioning is heavily influenced by the brain.

The brain is the quantitative factor; in computer terminology, it is the hardware system. Our brain functions more independently and is an objective instrument but has a genius for inaccuracy. It is "not a precise organ with standardized internal corrections for "reality." As extraordinary as it may seem, our brain is predisposed to generate three common mistakes.

The first mistake the brain makes is related to its perceptions for reality: What we see, hear, smell, and touch are merely a fractional, if not misleading, representation of the real world. Our perceptions are at best approximations.[9] The second mistake that the brain makes is in distinguishing things. It perceives independent entities or categories when such discrimination may be inaccurate and misleading. Eviatar Zerubavel suggests that in order to endow things with meaning, we manufacture such distinctions ("islands of meaning") in everyday life so as to establish order out of chaos. We will often bend our best thinking in order to force some perception into a comfortable, recognizable niche. This may also be a function of the brain's need for closure and avoidance of gaps.[10]

The third mistake that the brain makes is to contrast, that is, to accept an uncompromising black-and-white predisposition. In our brain, opposites are mutually exclusive: all things are either present or absent. Such either/or logic presupposes a digital mode of thinking, so that, in direct contrast to its analogue counterpart, the mind is unable to tolerate any shading among different mental fields. In this regard, digital thinking of the brain has been likened to the on/off feature of the conventional light switch, whereas analogue thinking of the mind is applicable to the function of a dimmer.[11]

The mind has no cells of its own but is able to communicate with thousands of other nerve cells in the brain. These cells are making trillions of connections simultaneously. They, however, do not directly deliver these messages; rather, they depend upon a type of chemical messenger known as a neurotransmitter. Neurotransmitters, of which there are many, occur at special junctures, the synapses. In the complex operation of the brain, every sensation or affect we experience and every action, however small, derives from these multitrillion physical encounters among axons and dendrites (both nerve cells) and neurotransmitters. Moreover, this physiological system is exquisite: these events occur, unrelentingly, every fraction of a second, within which information within the brain is processed, sent forth, and received.

The brain and its product, the mind, together, compound each other's limitations when it comes to verbalization—the final pathway of communication. There stands the ultimate source of misunderstanding between people when they negotiate "reality." The fact that there is no actual essence in words increasingly facilitates the possibility of ambiguities. At best words are our own reflection of this essence, whether we are discussing the weather, a movie, or our feelings. Each person thus creates his or her own system of language—a derivative of the communal one—and superimposes it upon presumed universal meanings. This is somewhat like the denotation (dictionary meaning) of a word differentiated from its connotation (what it means specifically to a specific person). Some people take this presumption to an extreme so that, to them, by having uttered a word, they think the occurrence or circumstance is real.[12] Russell Smith has said that since the concepts people live by are derived only from perceptions and from language we come "pretty close to living in the house that language built."[13]

When people complain about each other's communication, they may be caught in this language dilemma: language becomes gesture, whereby speakers charge their words with *meaning*. Nevertheless, language is fundamentally unstable and therefore, unstabilizing. Ludwig Wittgenstein says that language is, rather, a game where the competitors, by mutual agreement, that is, social convention, establish the rules.[14] Peter L. Berger has distinguished between two different types of reality:

> 'Cognitive reality' tells us what the world is like, whereas 'normative reality' tells us how to act. These distinctions are integrally related, however, in that all normative definitions derive from and depend upon specific cognitive definitions. . . . More aptly, the perceptual language of cognition, which informs us about reality (i.e., *what is*), must be unmistakable before we can examine the normative language of normality (i.e., *what ought to be*).[15]

The Bible provides us with a perfect example of a clash between these two different realities. Most likely it is neither intended to be such an example, nor to be humorous. "The total absence of humor from the Bible," said Alfred North Whitehead, "is one of the most singular things in the literature."[16]

Witness Nebuchandnezzar's dream about a statue made of four metals, as recorded in Daniel 2:1–9.

> Nebuchandnezzar, the King of Babylon during the second year of his reign of Jerusalem, experienced some troubling dreams. Although he slept, he was distressed and decided to send for his wizards—magicians, psychics, sorcerers, and astrologers—so that they could tell him about what he had dreamt. When they came to the king, he said he had had a dream and was troubled by it. He wanted to know what the dream meant.

> They answered the King, "Your Majesty, may you live forever! Tell us the dream, we'll interpret it for you."
>
> The King answered, "I mean what I said! If you don't tell me the dream and its meaning, you'll be torn limb from limb, and your houses will be turned into piles of rubble. But if you tell me the dream and its meaning, I will give you gifts, awards, and high honors. Now tell me the dream and its meaning" Once more they said to him, "Your Majesty, tell us the dream, and we'll tell you its meaning."
>
> The King, even more insistent, again replied, "I'm sure you're trying to buy some time because you know that I meant what I said. If you don't tell me the dream, you'll all receive the same punishment. You have agreed among yourselves to make up a phony explanation to give me, hoping that things will change. So tell me the dream. Then I'll know that you can explain its meaning."

There are bosses like Nebuchandnezzar.

Stress can also result from interactions between a stressor and an individual's perception and reaction. "When something happens, the only thing in your power is your attitude toward it... What really frightens and dismays us is not the external events themselves, but the way in which we think about them. It is not things that disturb us, but our interpretations of their significance," says ancient Greek (1st century A.D.) Stoic philosopher Epictetus, in his book *The Art of Living*.[17] Each stressor has its own cognate receptors, i.e., its neurochemical signature; each person has his/her own pattern of response and different stress triggers. Money and work problems seem to rank near the top, just below a serious illness. A life-endangering disease changes all equations. Being with a socially dominant person, experiencing role ambiguity, too much face time with the boss, or peer rejection (especially in adolescence), or even simply interrupting of one's peaceful routine are all enough to generate a high level of cortisol and impair cognitive performances.

For chronically anxious people (the worriers), there is always something that increases their cortisol level and creates omnipresent stress. According to an ancient fable, a mouse was in constant distress because of its fear of a cat. A magician took pity on it and turned it into a cat. But then it became afraid of a dog. So the magician turned it into a dog. Then it began to fear a panther. So the magician turned it into a panther. Whereupon it was full of fear for the hunter.[18]

An individual who is not a victim of philosophical dysphoria but possesses sufficient inner sustainment may induce the production of those above-mentioned wellness hormones and neurotransmitters by detoxifying the cortical system from its negative thoughts, feelings, and behavior and generate positive ones.

No one, however, is free from stress. Even God is burdened by daily pressure: "Besides those things that are outside, there is that which presses on me daily: anxiety for all the assemblies."[19] To live means to be subjected to stress. The purpose is not to eliminate stress totally, since that cannot be done; the purpose is to manage, to neutralize, or even to use stress to develop resilience. The ventromedial prefrontal cortex (PFC) appraises a threat and regulates the response. Greater PFC's resilience lessens the amydala's activity in response to negative stimuli.

The Bible describes how resilience can manifest itself under stress. "We are pressed on every side, yet not crushed; perplexed, yet not to despair."[20] A resilient person, even under the worst circumstances, can find life worth fighting for, even if briefly:

> A man traveling across a field encountered a tiger. He fled, the tiger after him. Coming to a precipice, he caught hold of the root of a wild vine and swung himself down over the edge. The tiger sniffed at him from above. Trembling, the man looked down to where, far below, another tiger was waiting for him. Only the vine sustained him. Then he saw a luscious strawberry near him. Grasping the vine with one hand, he plucked the strawberry with the other. How sweet it tasted!

People can be trained to be more resilient by modulating the brain's PFC activities. One may learn reappraisal of the stress, in order to tame the human mind's catastrophizing tendency. A Zen master says that by asking, "Is it really so?" One can reduce a lot of suffering. It is possible to stimulate oxytocin and neuropeptides by social activities, meditation, understanding the essence of impermanence and gaining a transcending attitude, a kind of philosophical reframing of one's world view.

Being physically and psychologically healthy requires cultivating the art of regulating our biological rhythm with the universe. The sun and moon "talk to" us through this universal rhythm. Health is a natural state of equilibrium, and left on its own, the body can most likely recover from its disequilibrium. But you can sometimes either make it worse or help out.

Stresses are intensified by our excessive and/or presumptive reactions. At times you need to let things take their course. A master says, let them fall into a timeless "Zen hole." Live in the present. The Bible says, "Don't be anxious for tomorrow, for tomorrow will be anxious for itself. Each day's own evil is sufficient."[21] As to the past, the only thing useful about it are the lessons drawn from it. Regrets, remorse, shame, guilt, (Spinoza's "les passions tristes")[22] related to the conviction of "I could have done better" or "differently" requires that you come to terms with your past to avoid lifelong philosophical, existential stresses. Emotions associated with trauma never totally disappear because it is as if our visceral brain never forgets; the content, though, will get blurry, distorted and may even be deleted (the cortical brain is a self-eraser over time). That is why the truth is more felt than known.

Focus not on what is wrong, but what is right in your life. You cannot always get rid of negatives, but you can add more positives; it is like planting pachysandras to the extent that there is no room left for weeds. Walk away from the stressful situation if feasible; do not fall into inertia, but rather move, and let the step ahead become the step behind. If your stress is the kind of stress you cannot put behind you, then embrace your life as is and learn to cope with it.

Shifting from the state of "doing" to the state of "being," creating solitude in nature, and forming a transcending philosophy of "oneness" with the world are three other significant ways of coping with stress.

A *being mode* involves a shifting from doing to being, from an efficient, accurate digital mode of operation to an inefficient analog mode of existence. Replace the verbs in the digital form of "should," "musts," and "have tos;" with the analog form of "is," "mays," and "mights." A being state is not a period of inactivity; one can be active in enriching and/or regenerative activities. You can listen to music, watch sports, read, visit museums, or see a performance; these are enriching enjoyments from without. The regenerative activities, such as painting, writing, playing musical instruments and doing sports, manifest from within.

We need social contact with others for our physiological up-regulation, but we also need to be alone for down-regulation. All human relationships are emotionally charged and thus have to be dosed at the level of our own unique personal tolerance. After any lengthy human encounter, most of us need to seek a sanctuary to allow sedimentation of our thoughts and emotions. Some intimate relations do not require that: those are the people who are able to be alone in each other's presence.[23]

In bullfighting arenas, there is a *querencia*—a safe spot set up for matadors to seek safety to pause and gather their strength before returning to the scene. For believers, God is such sanctuary. "God is refuge and strength, an ever-present help in trouble."[24] Everyone, i.e., believers and non-believers, need to set up a quiet and safe place to be alone and to recuperate from the stresses of daily life and emotionally be refueled.

In solitude, we don't need to do anything. Organisms seek their own equilibrium. All we need to do is to suppress all those disturbing thoughts and moods, stop discursive thinking, and cultivate a sense of retreat, i.e., a place where you can be within your own inner company. Our lives are so loaded with personal and business activities that most of us are never really alone. Social and professional obligations compound an already demanding family life so that we tend to find a sanctuary only in our sleep, if that. Solitude is replenishing. Occasionally, we need to reduce all stimuli. Susan Sontag talked about her own *attention surplus disorder* in Jill Krementz's *The Writer's Desk.*[25] Occasional *news-fast* is essential (negative material elicits more attention). Since we give ourselves about 20-30 thousand messages daily no matter how pleasant they may be, we need to experience a soundless, internal harmony of our own; we need to be mindful of our unfelt feelings, *unthought* ideas, and regroup our innate resources to bring cohesion into our scattered lives. Says Kierkegaard, in his book, *Either/Or,* "Most men pursue pleasure with such breathless haste that they hurry past it."[26]

Solitude in moments of uncommon *intuneness* is best attained within nature. Being alone, in a disciplined silence, is the practical way of calming both the body and mind; that is, withdraw from all stimuli, good and bad, and experience the warmth of silent communion with nature. That silence is the same in all tongues. In this primal solitude, you'll ascend to yourself. Listen to nature with an innerness that hovers beneath the surface. Yoga in Sanskrit means *unite with nature.* You can enter into your own native element in operative silence, if you allow yourself to be in communion with nature. Gently cradle yourself and find inner stillness within an unconstructive abandonment. There, a surprising calmness will wash over you, and your mind will slowly become still as the silence transforms into a harmonious and peaceful moment—a deep and abiding sense of wellness. You'll suddenly feel very light, clear, and deeply at peace. Such stillness of mind occasionally brings quantum leaps, not just on self-revelations, but also to creativity and problem-solving.

Buddha exhorts humanity to commune with nature; "If you wish to know the Divine, feel the wind on your face and the warm sun on your hand,"[27] hear the space between sounds and drift inward. Monks usually have a garden where they can walk in meditation. An individual can easily find a garden or a park where he/she can walk and meditate. The body is a walking tape recorder. Nature, as we walk within it, will dictate a soothing rhythm through natural sounds. They are like *niggunim* (wordless melodies). A Zen garden's "emptiness evoked by the sand, rocks, and plantings help clear the mind"[28] provided we actually dissolve in its mist and not just be an outside observer: touch, see, smell, and breathe them. Nature is a temple of gods; it is transformative. Kierkegaard writes, in his essay under his pseudonym, Johannes Climacus, "I observe nature in order to find God, and I do indeed see omnipotence and wisdom."[29]

Meditation as a psychological moratorium, a technique to break addiction to thinking is an effective de-stressor. You should have your own mantra to initiate and maintain your meditative concentration. The word *mantra* comes from two Sanskrit words: "man" means mind; "tra" means transporter. Your mantra transports your mind from an active to a quiescent state. A mantra's vibrating sounds, like *Omm*, will drift you away from the immediate into a timeless surrender.

> Mind is the activity in whose form awareness manifests and knows objective experience. Meditation is a relaxing of that activity, leaving awareness, its essential reality; standing alone in its original, naked, uncoloured, unmodulated condition—pure, luminous, empty knowing. Meditation is to be knowingly that luminous, open, empty, space-like presence of awareness, knowing its own aware being.[30]

Meditation at its best approximates a state of Nirvana. Nirvana is obtained not by seeing the world reflecting you and your possessions, but by seeing no reflection. Incidentally, *Nirvana* in Hindu means a mirror that no longer reflects any object—transcendence. Transcendental philosophy is the ultimate destressor—a liberation from time and space. It is a cultivation of spirituality—a form of intelligence, a profound engagement in a world: trusting only the ultimate healer, time. King Solomon asked one of his wisest advisors to design a ring with a saying that would always be true, so they put on it three words—"*gam zeh ya'avor*"—this too shall pass.[31] Physicist Carlo Rovelli, in his compelling *The Order of Time*, writes that we long for timelessness but permanence is only a "fleeting illusion."[32]

Such a transcending attitude can bring certain equanimity for bad times and equally importantly in good times. There is a Taoist story of an old farmer whose horse runs away. His neighbor sympathized with him. "What bad luck"; the farmer though, says "maybe." The following day the horse returned, bringing another horse, a wild one. The neighbor was happy for him: "What good luck," he said. The Farmer replied: "maybe."

The essence of transcendence is in understanding, i.e., really understanding, "It is here and it is now." We should not even be preoccupied with the present time; simply be present. Excessive future orientation generates anxiety. Excessive past orientation freezes us either in nostalgia, if the memories are positive; if the memories are negative, they sink us into chronic dysphoria. There is a charming Zen story about not being in the present.

> Two monks were once traveling together down a muddy road. A heavy rain was falling. Coming around the bend, they met a lovely girl in a silk kimono and sash, unable to cross the intersection. "Come on, girl," said the first monk. Lifting her in his arms, he carried her over the mud.
>
> The second monk did not speak again until that night when they reached the lodging temple. Then he no longer could restrain himself. "We monks don't go near females," he said. "It is dangerous. Why did you do that?"
>
> "I left the girl there," the first monk said. "Are you still carrying her?"[33]

The de-stressing philosophical attitude is learning to be *undifferentiated*. As early as the sixth century B.C., Pindar professed this sentiment: "Single is the race, single of men and gods; from a single mother we both draw breath."[34] Undifferentiation requires undoing self-differentiation, something that we have worked so hard to accomplish since very early childhood in the West. Undifferentiation is not losing our sense of self but recognizing how that self is very much part of a greater whole; it is feeling a boundless communion and understanding that we are all one. *"The universe is the divine womb"*[35] from which we all come, says Matthew Fox.

There is a tale of two young fish that were swimming by an old fish. The old fish asks how is the water? The young fish, puzzled, replies: 'What is water?' *Undifferentiation* is returning to this divine womb without even being so cognizant. We all drink from the same well. The Bible says all of us share one loaf.[36] We are all born from the same celestial seeds.[37] In short our human body is a universal body—a single unity.

The glue for this unity with the world is a state of mind that extends and dedifferentiates one from others, from things, and ultimately from the universe. John R. Howe, in *The Road Within*[38], talks about such enlarging boundaries: "a gradual but progressive growth of the self, incorporating within one's self the world outside. In short, the more individuals extend themselves, i.e., the more they embrace the universe, the less clear and less important are the distinctions between the self and the world. In fact, they may lose their boundaries and become totally identified with the world."[39]

In remembered oneness, all Gordian knots untie themselves.

NOTES

1. Carlo Rovelli, *The Order of Time*. (New York: Riverhead Books, an Imprint of Penguin Random House LLC, 2018), 166.

2. Viktor Frankl, *Man's Search for Meaning: An Introduction to Logotherapy*, 95.

3. Betty Friedan, *The Feminine Mystique* with an Introduction by Anna Quindlen, 249–251.

4. Alex Soojung-Kim Pang, *Rest* (New York: Basic Books, 2016), 3.

5. Mosiah 4:27.

6. Sylvia R. Karasu and T. Byram Karasu, *The Art of Marriage Maintenance*, 73.

7. Herbert Benson, *Timeless Healing: the Power and Belief* with Marg Stark (New York: Simon and Schuster, 1997), 128.

8. Sylvia R. Karasu and T. Byram Karasu, *The Art of Marriage Maintenance*, 184.

9. Sylvia R. Karasu and T. Byram Karasu, *The Art of Marriage Maintenance*, 74.

10. Sylvia R. Karasu and T. Byram Karasu, *The Art of Marriage Maintenance*, 75.

11. Sylvia R. Karasu and T. Byram Karasu, *The Art of Marriage Maintenance*, 76.

12. Sylvia R. Karasu and T. Byram Karasu, *The Art of Marriage Maintenance*, 77.

13. Russell F. W Smith, "Discussion: Linguistics in Theory—and in Practice." ETC: *Journal of Semantics* 10 (1) (Autumn 1952): 46–49.

14. Ludwig Wittgenstein, "Philosophical Investigations," in *Deconstruction in Context: Literature and Philosophy*, ed. Mark C. Taylor (Chicago: University of Chicago Press, 1986), 220–41.

15. Peter L. Berger, *A Far Glory* (New York: Macmillan, 1992), 193.

16. Alfred North Whitehead, *Dialogues of Alfred North Whitehead* As recorded by Lucien Price, editor (Boston: Little, Brown, 1954), 199.

17. Epictetus, "See Things for What They Are," in *The Art of Living: The Classical Manual on Virtue, Happiness, and Effectiveness* A New Interpretation by Sharon Lebell (New York: HarperOne, An Imprint of Harper Collins/Publishers, 1994), 7.

18. Anthony De Mello, *The Heart of the Enlightened* (New York: Doubleday, 1989), 16.

19. 2 Corinthians 11:28.

20. 2 Corinthians 4:8.

21. Matthew 6:34.

22. "Spinoza and *Les Passions Tristes*: Baruch Spinoza," in *Stanford Encyclopedia of Philosophy*: https://plato.stanford.edu/entries/spinoza/ Retrieved July 12, 2018.

23. D.W. Winnicott, "The Capacity to be Alone." *The International Journal of Psychoanalysis* (1958), 39:416–420.

24. Psalm 46:1–3.

25. Susan Sontag, Review of Jill Krementz's *The Writer's Desk* (New York: Random House, 1996, p. 17) Posted online by Pat Thomson, February 19, 2015. Retrieved July 10, 2018. http://world.edu/on-attention-surplus-disorder/.

26. Søren Kierkegaard, "Either/Or, A Fragment of Life, I" in *The Essential Kierkegaard*, ed. Howard V. Hong and Edna H. Hong (Princeton, NJ: Princeton University Press, 2000), 40–41.

27. Buddha, in Frederic Brussat and Mary Ann Brussat, *Spiritual Literacy: Reading the Sacred in Everyday Life* (New York: Touchstone, 1996), 121.

28. Thomas Moore, *A Religion of One's Own: A Guide to Creating a Personal Spirituality in a Secular World* (New York: Gotham Books/ Penguin, 2014), 242.

29. Søren Kierkegaard, "Concluding Unscientific Postscript to Philosophical Fragments: A Mimical-Pathetical-Dialectical Compilation, An Existential Contribution," by Johannes Climacus, ed. S. Kierkegaard in *The Essential Kierkegaard*, 207.

30. Rupert Spira, *The Nature of Consciousness: Essays on the Unity of Mind and Matter* (Oxford: Sahaja Publications, 2017), 80.

31. "This, Too, Shall Pass: King Solomon and the Ring," *Ask the Rabbi*, retrieved July 11, 2018. https://ohr.edu/ask_db/ask_main.php/335/Q1/.

32. Carlo Rovelli, *The Order of Time*, 191.

33. David Schiller, *The Little Zen Companion* (New York: Workman Publishing 1994), 359.

34. Pindar, "VI, 1–4," in *The Odes of Pindar*, trans. Cecil M. Bowra (Harmondsworth: Penguin Classics, 1969), 206.

35. Matthew W. Fox, *The Coming of the Cosmic Christ* (San Francisco: HarperCollins, 1988), 32.

36. 1 Corinthians 10:17.

37. Titus Lucretius Carus, *On the Nature of Things*, trans. Martin Ferguson Smith (Indianapolis: Hackett Publishing Company, Inc., 2001), 60.

38. John R. Howe, in *The Road Within: True Stories of Transformation* ed. Sean O'Reilly, James O'Reilly, and Tim O'Reilly (San Francisco: O'Reilly and Associates, 1997), 44.

39. T. Byram Karasu, *The Art of Serenity*, 157.

Lesson Six

Believe

Find a philosophy of life, and be meaningful

A metaphysical hunger for the frame that frames all frames
is an inherent ontological need in humans.

The human quest is not for the lost, but for the found, not for the known, but for the unknown: knowledge itself is a form of ignorance. Rewording Rupert Spira, all spiritual and religious paths, in one way or another, are aimed at expanding the mind beyond its limitations and seeking the unknown eternal, that is, its essential, irreducible reality.[1] These paths provide structures of belief systems: primarily the concept of God and its associated axioms. All religions share the same source—God—though they call that source with different names.

One useful image of the common ground of all religions was presented by the Christian, Bede Griffiths, who had spent most of his life in India. In a video interview made shortly before his death, he spread out his hand, saying religions are like separate fingers, quite distinct from each other. If you trace them to their source, however, you see that they all come together in the palm of your hand. Similarly, the thirteenth-century German mystic Meister Eckhart called God an underground river of wisdom with many wells tapping into it.[2]

"By definition a religion is something [centered] upon belief in the universe."[3] William James has written "Were one asked to characterize the life of religion in the broadest and most general terms, one might say that it consists in the belief that there is an unseen order, and that our supreme good lies in harmoniously adjusting ourselves thereto."[4] Richard Dawkins's "God Hypothesis" negates that "there exists a superhuman, supernatural intelligence who deliberately designed and created the universe and everything in it, including us."[5]

God is an easy target for phenomenological reductionism, He has been believed, denied, transcended but has always remained an ever-present subject in our lives. "God's death is always followed by his resurrection," says Carl Jung.[6]

Religion is *the opium of the people*;[7] for Karl Marx, religion was a veil that obscures all social and economic injustices. Many people believed that Marxism and Communism in Russia and China would make the concept of God irrelevant, at least in those countries. Even in the West, philosophers were convinced "atheism is demanded by the evolutionary theory."[8] They asserted that this illusion of the human mind, i.e., this learned ignorance, or bizarre invention, only serves bigotry and exploitation.

Algernon Charles Swinburne, an evangelist, who made the first credible secular leap of faith, made atheism his mission: God is not dead: he was never alive. Stop all these communal psychoses, he urged people, and focus on humanity rather than divinity.[9]

Scientists proclaimed that this is it, there is no "meta-narrative"; there is no other anticipated or as yet unrealized revelation.

They always argued about the lack of evidence of God's existence:

> There is a story about Bertrand Russell giving a public lecture somewhere or other in which he defended his atheism. A furious woman stood up at the end of the lecture and asked, "And Lord Russell, what will you say when you stand in front of the throne of God on Judgment Day?" Russell replied, "I will say: I'm terribly sorry, but you didn't give us enough evidence."[10]

This is a common way for atheists to react to religious claims: to ask for evidence, and often to reject these claims in its absence. Was Bertrand Russell a closet believer or did he just have a great sense of humor?

William James argues that God is a projection of specific psychological needs of individuals:

> One man allies it to the feeling of dependence; one makes it a derivative from fear; others connect it with the sexual life; others still identify it with the feeling of the infinite; and so on. Such different ways of conceiving it ought of themselves arouse doubt as to whether it can possibly be one specific thing . . . nothing whatever of a psychologically specific nature.[11]

In 1927, Sigmund Freud, in his book, *The Future of* Illusion,[12] argued that God and all related matters in religion were no more than infantile instinctual wishes and fears deliberately exploited by organized religion. Freud called religious doctrines "illusions," and he believed that they arose because of "our need to make our helplessness tolerable, especially against the forces of nature and the helplessness we experience in regard to our parents." For him, religion was an obsessional neurosis. In his essay *Leonardo da Vinci and a Memory of His Childhood*, Freud also explained, "A personal God is, psychologically, nothing other than an exalted father."[13] "If we attempt to assign the place of religion in the evolution of mankind, it appears not as a permanent acquisition but as a counterpart to the neurosis which individual civilized men have to go through in their passage from childhood to maturity."[14]

Early psychiatrists' and psychologists' contributions to the field are diverse and complementary. Freud offered insights into the role of the parents in the formation of the representation of God. Jung accumulated complex elaborations about religion, symbols, archetypes, and the archetype of the self. Alfred Adler converted God into a value. We can wonder whether patients analyzed by these therapists should be recalled.

Albert Camus argued that believing in God is tantamount to "philosophical suicide."[15] The eternity offered by any religion renders not only life but also death meaningless. Larkin says religion is a "vast moth-eaten musical brocade/Created to pretend we never die."[16]

There are the agnostics, who are either perplexed or simply display intellectual/political non-commitment; there are also the ambivalent atheists, who ironically pray to be free of God.[17]

Then, there is an ill-defined spirituality that embraces qualities of religious humanity without the operational aspects of God and religion. Spirituality is an individualized subjective experience, in contrast to religion's commonality and congregation. If spirituality tries a little harder, it may discover God.

Spirituality is an abstract concept devoid of doctrines and rituals; it is like a text without punctuations. Most religious people naturally consider themselves as spiritual, but spiritual people do not identify with any religion. Astrow and his colleagues define spirituality as "the search for transcendent meaning," which can be expressed as a "relationship to nature, music, the arts, a set of philosophical beliefs, or relationships with friends and family."[18] It is a yearning for direct connection to a harmony with the universe without any "intermediary."

Others do not believe in a god or spirituality but rather believe in a transcendental force in the universe. They experience the enormity of a starry night wherein time and space become one or none, *numinosity*. Albert Einstein gives a perfect example of such a perspective. He says: "I do not believe in a personal God and I have never denied this but have expressed it clearly. If something is in me which can be called religious then it is the unbounded admiration for the structure of the world so far as our science can reveal it."[19] Says Richard Dawkins, "The universe we observe has precisely the properties we should expect if there is, at bottom, no design, no purpose, no evil, no good, nothing but blind pitiless indifference."[20]

For philosopher Nietzsche, God is a harmful guest living in the human mind—"a thought which bendeth all that is straight."[21] "Do we still hear nothing of the noise of the gravediggers who are burying God? Do we smell nothing of the divine decomposition? Gods, too, decompose! God is dead! God remains dead! And we have killed him!"[22]

Nietzsche later in life reconsidered the consequences of his position and questioned whether the death of God was actually good news. "If God is dead, people would transfer their faith in God to something else. They had to believe in *something*."[23]

That "something" cannot be atheism because atheism is not exactly something; it is a philosophy that offers nothing. It is parasitic on religion; its content is determined by a negation of religion. It provides no alternative to fill the vacuum that it creates by negating God. Atheism is a derivative: its attraction resides primarily in what it denies and so it is hard to be enthusiastic about it. "Sermons on unbelief ever did attract me,"[24] said Emily Dickinson.

Undifferentiated Atheism, i.e. Humanism—the ethical system riding on atheism—and Secularism—all deprive the world of its literary aesthetics, and as the Archbishop of Canterbury, Rowan Williams, noted, they "[leave] us linguistically bereaved."[25]

High Trevor-Roper describes his sense of emptiness at a secular funeral:

> We stood silently around the coffin in the crematorium. No clergyman, no music, no articulate sound. Then suddenly the floor gaped and hey presto! The coffin sank out of sight. Whereupon we trooped silently away. I hope that my Doctorate of Divinity will at least save my corpse from such an undignified disposal: like waste going down the sink.[26]

Franz Kafka had a complex relationship to religion, says Guenther Anders. Kafka's themes included "guilt, redemption, grace, transcendence, absolute might, sacrifice—all categories that cannot be discussed for a moment outside the bounds of religious discourse."[27] Anders believes that Kafka's "entire work" can be understood in the light of the thesis, "God is dead;" Says Anders,

"…his doubts and despair never leave him…The prayer of one who prays in doubt becomes a poem."

Likewise, Albert Camus, in his later years, though not "primarily concerned with religion," was equally disillusioned by man's appropriation of divinity for himself. Camus, in his book *The Plague*, "attempts a parable about the human condition, an attack on the unthinking inauthenticity of most men's lives…and considers it a duty to bear witness…" to the injustices done to humans.[28] A little philosophy inclineth man's mind to atheism, says Francis Bacon "but depth in philosophy bringeth men's minds about to religion.[29]

Not only scientists and philosophers—non-overlapping *magisteria*—but all of us struggle with these questions: Is there a God? What is God? What is believing? What is the meaning of life? These are difficult questions. But any answerable question is worth asking. We don't even understand ourselves, let along God and life. Deepak Chopra makes a generic attempt: If one is convinced that there is something much greater than the human dimension, one is a believer.[30]

Without the burden of a reflective distance, believers find that the answers are included in the questions; these answers range from "*mu*" (meaning you've asked the wrong/ unanswerable/not applicable question) in the East, to "to serve God" in the West. In more puzzling moments, a faithful person is reconciled with "God knows!" Doubts, cognitive dissonances, ambivalences, and serious inquiries are left unindulged and kept in check by family and congregation. "Religious beliefs proper are always held by a defined collectivity that professes them and practices the rites that go with them."[31]

For true believers (i.e., undifferentiated theists of whatever religion), God and religion are transcending concepts. Alfred North Whitehead says:

> Religion is the vision of something which stands beyond, behind and within the passing flux of immediate things; something which is real, and yet waiting to be realized; something which is a remote possibility and yet the greatest of present facts; something that gives meaning to all passes and yet includes apprehension; something whose possession is the final good and yet is beyond all reach; something which is the ultimate ideal, and the hopeless quest.[32]

John Cottingham says religion offers "intimations of a transcendent world of meaning that breaks through into the ordinary world of our five senses."[33]

A believer's faith darkens when he or she experiences a serious trauma, such as losing a child, suffering a stroke, being diagnosed with cancer, or becoming a victim of a flood, fire, earthquake, or any other natural disaster. Even then, a believer will continue his belief. There is an old Jewish joke:

> A journalist, assigned to the Jerusalem bureau of his newspaper, had a room that overlooked the Wailing Wall. After several weeks, he became aware that regardless of the time of day, he always saw this old Jew praying vigorously at the wall. There must be a story here, he said. So he went down, introduced himself, and asked the old Jew what he was praying for. "What am I praying for?" In the morning I pray for world peace. Then I pray for the eradication of illness and disease from the earth, and at the end of the day I pray for the brotherhood of man." The journalist was very much taken by the old Jew. "You come every day to the wall and pray for these

> things?" Amazing. How long have you been praying here at the wall for these things?" The old Jew replied he had been praying here for 20 years. In awe of his devotion, the journalist asked, "And how does it feel to have prayed all these years for these wonderful things?" To which the old Jew replied, "How does it feel? It's like talking to a wall."[34]

A true theist (*a priori* a believer of his religion's "truth") remains comforted by his faith: To paraphrase François de La Rochefoucauld's[35] remark with regard to passions—just as the small fire is extinguished by the storm, a large fire is enhanced by it—likewise a weak faith is weakened by predicaments and catastrophes whereas a strong faith is strengthened by them. Again we find "*mu*" or "It is God's will," or "God has His mysterious ways." Any further questioning of theists' beliefs can run the risk of infinite regress. They do not hear the "what," "how," or "why;" they only want to hear the confirmation that "it is." God starts where common sense ends.

The "whole" in any field may be understood by learning its part, except in the field of divinity. You can understand only its part by understanding it as a whole. The word *understanding* here is less a cognitive phenomenon than a form of submission.

Those who live a life of faith stick to their world-view no matter how negating or disappointing the facts are. Francis Spufford laments about the quandary of subjective certainty in passionate inwardness:

> You ask for help and you get nothing: on a conscious level you may have decided that there was nobody there to help, but less consciously, since you did ask, it feels as if help was denied. Hence the angry edge that something sharpens disbelief when it's been

> renewed by one of these episodes of fruitless asking. In the words of Samuel Beckett, "He doesn't exist, the bastard!" The life of faith has just as many he-doesn't-exist-the bastard moments as the life of disbelief. Probably more of them, if anything, given that we believers tend to return to the subject more often, producing many more opportunities to be disappointed.[36]

Such a strong belief is rarely cultivatable in adults who did not get religious grounding in early childhood. Like our maternal language, the concept of God is learned by osmosis within a context of a religious family and upbringing, only in imprinted stages.

> There is a story of a tourist in India who notices an adult elephant was being held by a tiny rope tied to one of his ankles. The animal didn't move, though he could easily break away from its captivity. Surprised, the tourist asked the elephant trainer how that was possible. The trainer explained that when the elephants were young, the trainers used the same small rope to hold them, and it was sufficient. As the elephants grew up, they still believed that they could not break away.

For believers, God is intimately involved in all human affairs. He answers prayers, forgives or punishes sins, and intervenes in the world by performing miracles. God addresses not only the yearnings of people for the divine; He is equally vital for confirming and validating religious values and providing practical meaning for their lives. Faith is an ascent of the mind that lowers the heavens to earth.

As to non-believers, they are not immune from that "metaphysical hunger:" a being in search of *the Being*, i.e., a grasping for ecstatic knowledge "an ontological passion" with different manifestations. We see it "in the Platonic *eros* yearning for the Idea, the Stoic drive for wisdom, the Augustinian longing for truth itself, the *amor dei intellectualis* of Spinoza, and the Hegelian passion for the absolute."[37] With the exception of a true believer's comfort with the quantum unknowing, the quest to know is a human yearning, especially to know what frames all frames.

Belief in God is an inherent ontological need in humans. E. O. Wilson writes, "The predisposition to religious belief is the most complex and powerful force in the human mind and in all probability an ineradicable part of human nature."[38] We are prestructured, wired to believe. Voltaire built a chapel at Ferney with the inscription "Deo Erexit Voltaire" inscribed on the lintel and went so far as to suggest that if God had not existed it would have been necessary to invent him.[39] Aren't all temples built by man?

Neuro-theologists assert that there is even a biological basis for it. Dean Hamer, a researcher at the National Institutes of Health, has identified a "God gene" that codes for a brain receptor that regulates serotonin and dopamine and correlates with feelings of self-transcendence.[40] The brain areas associated with social categories (prefontal cortex), i.e., empathy (insula and anterior cingulate cortex), and face perception (fusiform face area), are also active during a variety of religious practices such as meditation and prayer.[41] Various fMRI studies suggest that the amygdala, the insula, and the area between the limbic system and the cortex, are the processors of emotional contents of beliefs, and GABA (Gamma-aminobutyric acid) may be their principal neurotransmitter. Meditation and prayer calm the parasympathetic system, lowering the heart rate and blood pressure, and shallow our breathing. Meditation and prayer increase beta-endorphins—the natural opioids produced by the hypothalamus that reduce fear and pain; they also stimulate oxytocin production and thus facilitate social bonding.

A spiritual experience is sort of a love of universal consciousness that borders on ecstasy. It seems to trigger activation of the amygdala with its somatic markers. It is possible that while spiritual moments may elicit dopamine with short-term highly positive emotions, religion may increase serotonin for tamed long-term positive experiences.

Questions arise about the presence of a soul; is the soul another name for the mind and can it be reduced merely to brain functions? The argument suggests that the soul is a property that emerges out of the complex workings of the brain but emerges as an independent property. Andrew Newberg offers an eloquent compromise: "An emergent property is something like "wetness" for water. We could not say that five molecules of H_2O are wet, but billions of molecules do have wetness. Similarly, one or two neurons firing do not explain the soul, but perhaps billions firing in concert can somehow precipitate a soul."[42]

Clashes between visions and belief systems cannot be settled by simple appeals to scientific evidence, especially since science itself delivers only interim reports. Even if we cultivate metaphysical minds, that is to say, become comfortable about entertaining religious and philosophical paradigms simultaneously, we will still get confused, occasionally partly because we think that we should not be confused. Our own phenomenal reality—some things that we can know and experience—may be less confusing even if they were not real. But there is also *noumenal* reality, the reality that we cannot know and experience. *Noumenal* reality, obviously, confuses everyone. Any pretention of knowing the unknowable is dangerous to one's self. Simply knowing the potentially knowable is hard enough. Chuang Tzu, for example, is considered a brilliant Chinese philosopher from the 4th century B.C., about whom not much is known. In his collected writings of anecdotes and fables, he writes that he and his friend Hui Tzu were walking along a riverbank.

> "How delightful the fishes are enjoying themselves in the water," Chuang Tzu exclaimed. "You are not a fish," his friend said. "How do you know whether or not the fishes are enjoying themselves?" Chuang Tzu said, "You are not me, how do you know that I couldn't know that the fishes are enjoying themselves."[43]

Non-believers who yearn for some anchoring need to domesticate the question: either they have to believe the unbelievable á la Tertullian's avowal: "The Son of God died; it is by all means to be believed, because it is absurd. And He was buried and rose again; the fact is certain because it is impossible."[44] And they have to accept the ultimate cognitive predicaments: the best evidence of God's existence is his absence—*"the ability to think of what is not."*[45] Or they have to transcend from a "subject theology" to a "predicate theology" and believe in the attributes of God, as divinity, and not in the subject *God.*

This concept of *Predicate Theology* has its origin in 19th-century German philosopher Ludwig Feuerbach. "Not the attribute of divinity but the divinity of the attribute is the first truly divine being."[46] Meditative reading of the scripture, *Lectio Divina*, can bring any non-dogmatic person to the same conclusion. Rabbi Harold M. Schulweis, who coined the term "predicate theology"[47] and who was primarily interested in theodicy, i.e., trying to reconcile the evil and the moral ideal of God, liked Feuerbach's call for this inversion of a religious concept and made it a proper subject of theology—"Predicate Theology."

Theological statements are traditionally expressed in terms of subject-predicate relations. However God is portrayed, whether as

Person, Being, or Power, theologians speak of Him as a subject to which there is attached a number of qualities: love, mercy, compassion, truthfulness, etc. These predicates are more or less identical in all religions. The Predicate theologist reverses these subject-predicate relationships: It is not "God is love," but it is rather "love is God;" it is not "God is mercy;" it is "mercy is God"; it is not "God is truth," but "truth is God;" it is not "God is compassion," but "compassion is God."

Following this inversion, we can shift our focus from the discussion of the existence or non-existence of God, to qualities attributed to God i.e. goodness, love, intelligence, and creativity. These are the qualities that are worthy of cultivation and emulation.

Attributes of religion and God are separate but highly intertwined. Attributes of religion pull us down to earth, and their purpose is to civilize humanity. Attributes of God pull us up to the Heavens, and their purpose is to make humans godly.[48] In tandem, they make us soulful and spiritual beings, and they provide meaning to our lives.[49] These grounding predicates of God and religion also offer a remedy for the common cognitive dissonance between organized religion and our need to be true to ourselves.

What matters most, says philosopher Ronald Dworkin, is the "conviction that there is, independently and objectively, a right way to live."[50] Predicate theology is hetero-normative. Those who have recovered from their primitive innocence need to formulate their ideas of God, regardless of their congregational affiliation. Some may not even need or want to be a part of a religion or a community. Isaac Bashevis Singer, the Nobel Prize winner in literature, was once asked, in an interview with Professor Richard Burgin, to which school of literature he belonged. He replied, "only small fish swim in schools."[51] Some individual who transcends the need to believe and belong may be such a "big fish." Happy swimming!

The rest may need to resonate emotionally with the God of their religion, but intellectually need to transcend all its dogma and cultivate a personal concept of a divinity free from any theological structure. Like the preliminary stammering of an orchestra with its exploratory notes, this transition may generate a few discordant moments within, before all can develop perfect harmony. A person so enlightened achieves enduring equanimity by striving to own the attributes of God—to be godly. "What is the good of a man," asks D.H. Lawrence, in his poem *Glimpses,* written in his later years, "unless there's the glimpse of a god in him and her?"[52]

I traveled a long way seeking God, says Zen master, and finally I found myself.

NOTES

1. Rupert Spira, *The Nature of Consciousness: Essays on the Unity of Mind and Matter*, 53.
2. Frederic Brussat and Mary Ann Brussat, *Spiritual Literacy: Reading the Sacred in Everyday Life*, 18.
3. A.C. Grayling, *Against All Odds* (London: Oberon Books, 2007), 29.
4. William James, *The Varieties of Religious Experience* (New York: Longmans, Green, 1902), 53.
5. Richard Dawkins, *The God Delusion* (London: Bantam, 2006), 52.
6. Carl Jung quoted in Alister McGrath, *The Twilight of Atheism*, (New York: Doubleday, 2006), 189.
7. Karl Marx, "A Contribution to the Critique of Hegel's Philosophy of Right," *Deutsch-Französische Jahrbücher, February 1844,* Marxists

Internet Archive, retrieved June 29, 2018. https://www.marxists.org/archive/marx/works/1843/critique-hpr/intro.htm.

8. Alister McGrath, *The Twilight of Atheism*, (New York: Doubleday, 2004), 108.

9. Algernon Charles Swinburne, "Hymn of Man," in *The Poems of Algernon Charles Swinburne in Six Volumes, Vol. 2,* ed. John A. Walsh, (London: Chatto and Windus, 1904), 93–104.

10. Tim Crane, *The Meaning of Belief: Religion from an Atheist's Point of View*, (London, Harvard University Press, 2017), 65.

11. William James, *The Varieties of Religious Experience*, 27.

12. Sigmund Freud. "The Future of an Illusion," in *The Standard Edition of the Complete Psychological Works of Sigmund Freud Volume XXI,* trans. and ed. James Strachey, in collaboration with Anna Freud, Alix Strachey and Alan Tyson (London: The Hogarth Press, 1968), 18, 21, 33, 43.

13. Sigmund Freud, "Leonardo da Vinci and a Memory of His Childhood," in *The Freud Reader*, ed. Peter Gay (New York, NY: W.W. Norton and Company, Inc., 1989), 474.

14. Sigmund Freud, *New Introductory Lectures on Psychoanalysis*, trans. and ed. James Strachey (New York: W.W. Norton & Company, Inc., 1965), 168.

15. Albert Camus, "The Myth of Sisyphus" in *The Myth of Sisyphus and Other Essays* (New York: Vintage Books, 1991), 41.

16. Philip Larkin, "Aubade," in *Collected Poems*, ed. Anthony Thwaite (London: Faber and Faber, 2003), 208.

17. Meister Eckhart, *Meister Eckhart: The Essential Sermons, Commentaries, Treatises, and Defense*, trans. Edmund Colledge and Bernard McGinn (New York: Paulist Press, 1981), 202.

18. A. Astrow, C. Pulchalski, D Sulmasy "Religion, spirituality, and health care: Social, ethical, and practical considerations," *American Journal of Medicine* 110 (2001): 283–287.

19. Albert Einstein, "*Letter to Joseph Dispentiere on March 24, 1954*," Wikipedia, last modified March 24, 2016. https://en.wikipedia.org/wiki/Religious_views_of_Albert_Einstein.

20. Richard Dawkins, *River out of Eden: A Darwinian View of Life*, (New York: Basic Books, 1995), 133.

21. Friedrich Nietzsche, *Thus Spake Zarathustra: A Book for All And None*, trans. Alexander Tille, (New York: The MacMillan Company, 1896), 116.

22. Friedrich Nietzsche, *The Gay Science*, ed. Bernard Williams, trans. Josefine Nauckhoff, (New York: Cambridge University Press, 2001), 119–120.

23. Alister McGrath, *Twilight of Atheism*, 262.

24. Emily Dickinson in Richard Benson Sewall, *The Life of Emily Dickinson*, (Cambridge, MA: Harvard University Press, 1974), 462.

25. Archbishop Rowan Williams, "Raymond Williams Lecture" (Hay Festival, Wales, UK, June 1, 2002).

26. High Trevor-Roper, *One Hundred Letters from Hugh Trevor-Roper*, ed. Richard Davenport-Hines (Oxford: Oxford University Press, 2014), 349.

27. Guenther Anders, "Kafka: Ritual Without Religion: The Modern Intellectual's Shamefaced Atheism." *Commentary* 8 (1949): 560–569.

28. Walter Kaufman, ed. *Religion from Tolstoy to Camus* with a new introduction by Paul Gottfried, *Introduction*, (London: Routledge: Taylor & Francis Group, 1994), 1–44.

29. Francis Bacon, *The Philosophical Works of Francis Bacon*, ed. J.M. Robertson (New York: E.P. Dutton & Co., 1905), 754.

30. Deepak Chopra, personal communication.

31. Émile Durkheim, *The Elementary Forms of Religious Life* (1912; repr., Oxford: Oxford University Press, 2001), 42.

32. Alfred North Whitehead, *Science and the Modern World* (1925; repr., New York: Free Press, 1967), 192.

33. John Cottingham, *The Meaning of Life* (London: Routledge, 2003), 100.

34. "Talking to the Wall," Humor Planet, retrieved on July 10, 2018. https://www.humorplanet.com/joke.cgi?category=religion&joke=10.

35. Francois Duc De La Rochefoucauld, Prince de Marsillac, *Reflections: or Sentences and Moral Maxims,* translated from the Editions of

1678 and 1827 by J.W. Bund and J. Hain Friswell (London: Simpson Low, Son, and Marston, 188, Fleet Street, 1871), retrieved on July 8, 2018. http://www.gutenberg.org/files/9105/9105-h/9105-h.htm.

36. Francis Spufford, *Unapologetic: Why, Despite Everything, Christianity Can Still Make Surprising Emotional Sense* (London: Faber and Faber, 2013), 68.

37. Harold Schulweis, *Evil and the Morality of God* (Jersey City: KTAV Publishing House, 2010), 16.

38. E. O. Wilson, *On Human Nature* (Cambridge: Harvard University Press, 1978), 169.

39. Karen Armstrong, *A History of God: The 4,000-Year Quest of Judaism, Christianity, and Islam* (New York: Ballantine Books, 1993), 310.

40. Dean Hamer, *The God Gene: How Faith is Hardwired into Our Genes* (New York: Random House, 2004), 11–12.

41. Andrew Newberg, *Neurotheology How Science Can Enlighten Us About Spirituality* (New York: Columbia University Press, 2018) 114.

42. Andrew Newberg, *Neurotheology How Science Can Enlighten Us About Spirituality*, 103.

43. Chuang Tzu. *The Complete Works of Chuang Tzu*. Translated by Burton Watson. (New York: Columbia University Press, 1968), 188–189.

44. Tertullian, "Chapter V. Christ Truly Lived and Died in Human Flesh: Incidents of His Human Life on Earth, and Refutation of Marcion's Docetic Parody of the Same," in *On the Flesh of Christ* (Minnesota: Lighthouse Publishing, 2015), 15.

45. J.P. Sartre, *The Psychology of the Imagination* (London: Methuen and Co., Ltd., 1972), passim, in Karen Armstrong, *A History of God: The 4,000-Year Quest of Judaism, Christianity, and Islam*, 233.

46. Ludwig Feuerbach, *The Essence of Christianity*, trans. George Eliot (London: John Chapman, 1890), xviii.

47. Harold Kushner, about Harold Schulweis, in *Who Needs God.* (New York: Pocket Books, 1991), 203.

48. T. Byram Karasu, "Of God and Psychotherapy," *American Journal of Psychotherapy* 69(4): 357–360, 2015.

49. Thomas Moore, *Care of the Soul* (New York: Harper Perennial, 2016). Retrieved July 11, 2018. https://www.amazon.com/Care-Soul-Twenty-fifth-Anniversary Cultivatingebook/dp/B01AFYCPMG/ref=sr_1_1_atc_badge_A28VFQ2RQJP1YP_twi_kin_2?ie=UTF8&qid=1531344681&sr=81&keywords=care+of+the+soul+by+thomas+moore#reader_B01AFYCPMG.

50. Ronald Dworkin, *Religion Without God* (Cambridge: Harvard University Press, 2013), 155.

51. Isaac Bashevis Singer, "Only Small Fish Swim in Schools," Posted online by Michael Jinkins, February 20, 2018. "Isaac Bashevis Singer on the Joy of Reading." Retrieved July 10, 2018. http://www.lpts.edu/about/our-leadership/president/thinking-out-loud.

52. D.H. Lawrence, "Glimpses," in *The Complete Poems of D.H. Lawrence*. (Hertfordshire: Wordsworth Editions Limited, 2002), 561.

Lesson Seven

Be

Cultivate an inner communion, and be joyful

Being joyful is one of the most significant human qualities for creating a sense of wellbeing for self and others. It is a much-appreciated asset in social, personal, and professional contexts. We all like and are drawn to those who are really joyful. Social charm, cheerfulness and smiles, as pleasant as they are, may not necessarily reflect a person's inner state. "The act" of social exuberance is commonly related to one's various agendas i.e. acceptance, seduction, deal-making, etc. This outer attitude—*the persona*—though, may be different from the inner attitude—*the anima*.

Though many use a ghostwriter, every human being is the author of his/her higher persona, not his/her anima. *Anima* is not authorable; it is natural and evolving, with no end point. In that sense, no one is truly himself, but just becoming. The only thing you can know for sure—at any given moment is that you exist. It has been said that we are all born originals but often live as copies. Some people cultivate the art of counterfeiting themselves: they are no more than their persona—a sum of their impersonations, with or without moral mutations. Like the character of the mime Marcel Marceau, they cannot take off that last mask. Their acts are situation-specific and time-limited; they display contrasting reversal of moods similar to Broadway actors who look totally drained after two hours of acting certain roles. Only an inner attitude of a person remains stable, in all contexts, including and especially in solitude.

The desire for "happiness" is a gravitational pull of our nature; happiness, though, is so indistinct that we are pulled in all directions. For example, philosopher Jeremy Bentham pulls us into his observational definition of happiness—securing five elements in living:

> 1. Securing to the possessor a proportionable share of *general respect*. . . . 2. Security against *ennui*, viz, the condition of him who, for want of something in prospect that would afford him pleasure, *knows not what to do with himself*, a malady to which, on retirement, men of business are particularly exposed. . . . 3. Security against *inordinate sensuality*, and its mischievous consequences. 4. Security against *idleness*, and consequent *mischievousness*. . . . 5. Security for admission into, and agreeable intercourse with, *good company*: i.e. company in, or from which, present and harmless pleasure, or future profit or security, or both, may be obtained.[1]

Jeremy Bentham's path to happiness is too empirical and self-oriented to be adequate. Daniel Haybron pulls us into an emotionally complex, self-affirmatory state:

> it involves three broad categories of affective state, including *endorsement* states like joy versus sadness, *engagement* states like flow or a sense of vitality, *and attunement* states like tranquility,

> emotional expansiveness versus compression, and confidence. Given the departures from commonsensical notions being in a "good mood," happiness is characterized in this proposal as "psychic affirmation," or "psychic flourishing" in pronounced forms.[2]

Haybron's path to happiness remains too qualified to be useful. Utilitarian John Stuart Mill pulls us out of ourselves:

> "Those only are happy (I thought) who have their minds fixed on some objects other than their own happiness: on the happiness of others, on the improvement of mankind, even on some art or pursuit, followed not as a means, but as an ideal end. Aiming thus at something else, they find happiness by the way."[3]

John Stuart Mill's path to happiness is a little too altruistic for Western societies. For Utilitarians, joyfulness depends on a promised convergence of personal and general happiness. But even relative success of such self-denial demands an enormous compromise. The utilitarian definition of happiness is akin to a platonic reordering of the self.

These are just a few of the innumerable definitions of happiness. Everyone seems to have his/her own ill-defined definition of "happiness" for which no unanimous description emerges. In fact drastically, the chorus of Oedipus calls no man happy until he is dead.

Books on happiness (and there is a whole body of literature on it) merely cultivate at best a healthy narcissism in individuals. On the other hand, the word "joy" has been totally relegated to devotional literature. Joyfulness, i.e., that the main source of a sense of well-being, is understated and underappreciated, if not dismissed. Healthy narcissism-fueled "happiness," derived from something outside of us, offers delight for our mind and body.

Joyfulness arises within us. The former may bring pleasure and even counterfeit ecstasy but no inner sustainment whereas the latter bears intense invigoration.

In *The Book of Joy*, Dalai Lama and colleagues praise the calmness of joy over raucous happiness.[4] A religion's path to happiness/joyfulness is enigmatic. Religions advise their adherents to be joyful. The Bible says, "Always rejoice."[5] In fact, the word "joy" is mentioned one hundred sixty-four times in the Bible. Buddhism connects joyfulness to a purity of thoughts, "Joy follows a pure thought like a shadow that never leaves."[6]

Most religions connect the secret of joyfulness to believing in and praising their version of God. For a true believer, this formula may be a ready-made solution for the question of "how to be joyful:" centering on God. For the non-believer, though, such "God-centering" only brings an impasse of "false decentering," an inauthentic averageness that renders the nucleus of the self vulnerable. For a non-believer, becoming joyful demands genuine self-decentering.

Some people don't even self-center, let alone experience a joyful decentering. They spend their days in an "observer-participating role" in other people's lives and *in alio*, i.e. inhabiting the discourse of others (more suitable role for priests, ministers, and psychotherapists), and never *in se*, i.e., living their own true lives. Those who have not centered cannot de-center. True self-decentering first requires the knowledge of "the self." There you will be your own point of reference, and you will be the center of all your own doing, the way a dancer takes her center with her—a moving matrix. "I" is the common element in all of our experiences; in fact "I" is the *Prima materia* experience. Author Stephen R. Covey writes: "Each of us tends to think we see things as they are, that we are objective. But this is not the case. We see the world, not as it is, but as we are—or, as we are conditioned to see it. When we open our mouths to describe what we see, we, in effect, describe ourselves, our perceptions, our paradigms."[7]

In the ordeal of the self, there is no rescue by immunity. The evolution of a true self—anchoring in depth, is the only kind of salvation, with joyfulness to follow. Rewording the *Mill Principle* "only the fullest self-development of one's potential gives access to the highest forms of human happiness."[8]

Common happiness is a result of various forms of successes—both ascensions and a litany of contentment. This outward journey ultimately wears itself out, and then an inward transcending one must beckon. This process begins with the person's becoming an authentic and mature adult: "The path to sainthood goes through adulthood," says M. Scott Peck.[9] There is no path to happiness; happiness is the path—a path to joyfulness. But do not be scared; no one expects you to be a saint. As to adulthood, everyone becomes grown up at his or her own pace. Only those who make nothing happen too slowly will end up suffering from an adult developmental arrest.

To know oneself requires the development of self-relatedness, i. e., having an internal dialogue by being both the subject and the "object of experience" simultaneously. People tend to relate to themselves mostly in the mode of self-avoidance: they never get to know themselves and are never known by others. Only when you cultivate self-awareness, and know yourself, will you then be known.

Self-awareness initially generates a divine discontent, a formless anxiety, and one may look for temporary fusions to eradicate it. But if self-awareness is so aborted—not carried to term—anxiety can become chronic and these temporary fusions transform themselves into full dependency. Such a person will end up having a perfunctory, provisionary existence—a malpractice of life.

Some people are "as if" people: they live their lives as though living with a stranger. They inhabit a host of ideas, feelings, and actions that are mostly fed by others. Some of them present themselves with a chronic inchoate suffering of *weltschmerz* (world pain)—an inner inquietude that usually leads to false solutions. Still some others enter wrong paths, and from then on, one wrong outcome follows another. In one of his lectures, Bernard Malamud said that if your train is on the wrong track, every station you come to is the wrong station. Some people are always taking the wrong trains, others are often missing their trains, and still others are just train watchers, coasting through life. Then there are those who are carried by others.

In a Zen story, a horseman was galloping through a village, "Where are you going in such a hurry, asked a bystander. "I don't know," shouted the horseman. "Ask the horse!"

You have to take charge of your life fully and know exactly where you are going. If you don't know where you are going, then any horse or any train will take you there.

Frequently, we may be puzzled by our own decisions or behavior. We may regret our missed opportunities or damages that we have inflicted on loved ones; equally we may wonder about unusual generosities we have bestowed on others. All these seemingly unanswerable questions are related to our lack of self-awareness. Knowing yourself will help you ask the right questions, and more importantly, bring these questions down to a level of answerability. In the following story, an answer to an unanswerable question leaves both parties puzzled:

Every morning a mufti watched a mystic who sat in the mosque and prayed aloud: "God please open the door," he said weeping, as tears rolled down his face, "God, please let me in." The mufti finally lost his patience, went and sat next to him and said "Stop all this nonsense; the door is open, and in fact, you are already in." The mystic looked at the mufti totally puzzled.

A person's authenticity, i.e., self-harmony, requires approximation of his/her outer and inner attitudes. To find your authentic self, you need to break away from your definition by others. "Only God knows our real name"[10] says James Hillman, dramatizing the difficulties of self-knowledge. To find out who you are begins with self-transparency. You need to stop doing and saying things that are not exactly who you are. What is false in you will falsify your entire life. A simple pausing or a period of self-reflection can serve as the prism for seeking an inner communion. The frontiers of enlightenment and joyfulness lie within.

Self-transparency is finding your way back to yourself again, a kind of giving birth to yourself. It is stripping down to your bare essence by shedding all inauthentic layers and regaining a lost innocence. Donna Schaper[11] compares such self-stripping to scraping the varnish off an old wooden chair. For a moment you may feel a little too naked and confused. Let it be: usually, puzzlement precedes enlightenment.

Only after you have reached your "raw" essence, can your healthy psychological birth begin. There are no psychological supermodels to emulate. You need not to be any more than becoming yourself—your authentic self.

On his deathbed, the mystic Zusia lamented and trembled with the fear of facing God. He was prepping himself to answer what he

> assumed to be God's questions, such as "Why were you not like Moses, or at least like Rabbi Akiba?" Zusia thought he would say: "God, you never gave me the qualities of being like them." What if God, though, asks him. "How come you never became Zusia? I gave you all the qualities of being Zusia."

Keats writes, "Unweave a rainbow" as it made his "tender-person'd Lamia melt into a shade."[12] Rather, unlike Keats, *weave* your own rainbow, and emerge into a bright sunshine. You are given all the qualities of yourself. So become yourself.

We all acquire only degrees of being. Even then, self-awareness is a cross-sectional moment in a stream of ongoing existence. Everyone has his/her own timetable and pace of becoming, and it is commonly a slow process: there are no microwave equivalents, although occasionally some quantum leaps occur. Either way if you are so committed, you'll find yourself unfolding into wholeness.

This "becoming real" is not about normality; it is about "realness." Too much emphasis has been put wrongly on normality, a pathology itself, i.e., the pathology of normality—a social tyranny. There is no norm for normality. In fact, normality itself is a spectrum disorder.

Becoming real is becoming an authentic being, having an authentic mind. An authentic mind consistently monitors itself, especially when it attempts to go beyond its enclosure and attempts to transcend it. But in order to transcend, one has to have something to transcend. That is why an inauthentic, unformed mind that seeks transcendence at the feet of a Tibetan guru will be no more formed than before. The self that you find at the mountaintop is the "same self [you] took up there."[13] The authentic, well-formed, self-congruent, coherent, and cogent state of mind represents the base. Then, only after then, can you aspire to a philosophy of goodness—the true source of joyfulness.

Joyfulness of the authentic, Eudemonism, is a byproduct of "goodness," universal benevolence, and calm self-love. Goodness is the endpoint, says John Skorupski:

> (i) There is a system of agent-neutral final ends (the Good). . . . (ii) There are no complete agent-relative telic reasons. (iii) There are no complete non-telic reasons. This is, of course, simply a slightly technical way of saying that the best action is one that promotes the most Good and that all practical reasons are Good-based, that is, that when spelled out they are instances of the principle of Good.[14]

There are a number of fundamental elements of joyful goodness, such as morality, humility, kindness, compassion, optimism, and simplicity, that every culture and religion consider worthy of cultivating. These qualities of goodness are recognized as direct lines to joyfulness but are not necessarily the only ones. The most common way to write music is on *staves*—five horizontal lines. Notes are placed on one of these lines. Extra lines may be added to show that a note is too high or too low on the staff, the singular of staves. As your wisdom sediments, you may experience other traits above and below these common lines, just like a master composer. Transcendence occurs paradoxically in a nascent state, in low staves.

Whether there can be such qualities as goodness without religion has been long debated. If human morals and values do not arise out of belief in God, where will they come from? Paul Kurtz replies, "They come from our common humanity"[15]—a rational morality. *Rational morality* is a code of values required by us for our and others' well-being. Such a code is based on the essence of human values, a kind of *meta-ethics*. Conscience is the self's judgment: an inner tribunal. These moral standards are universal. Anthropologist Solomon Asch, in his work *Social Psychology* says: "We do not know of societies in which bravery is despised and cowardice held up to honor, in which generosity is considered a vice and ingratitude a virtue."[16]

Historically, religions articulate those cultural moral values. Cultures and religions are highly intertwined and have similar codes of behavior for their subjects and adherents: Be honest, be respectful, forgive wrongdoings, do not lie, do not kill, do not commit adultery, do not steal, and do no harm. These dictates are not merely about conformity to moral law; they also espouse moral ideals that religions promote, sometimes poetically. Sin, though, exiles a man from himself.

Even the language for codes of behavior in various religions and cultures is remarkably similar. For example, the Bible says, "Therefore whatever you desire for men to do to you, you shall also do to them."[17] In *The Doctrine of the Mean* 13.3, written about 500 B.C., Confucius said, "What you do not like when done to yourself, do not do to others."[18] Isocrates (c.375 B.C.) said,"Do not do to others that which angers you when they do it to you."[19] The Hindu *Mahabharata*, circa150 BC, teaches, "This is the sum of all true righteousness: deal with others as thou wouldst thyself be dealt by."[20] The formative self-cultivation of Confucians has included, for example, rituals "designed to create a *junzi*, a mature fully developed human being who did not treat others carelessly, perfunctorily, or selfishly."[21] Incidentally, all religious demands, including the 10 commandments, are not unattainable. For example, there is no commandment like "don't eat!" at least not for too long.

Humility and simplicity are two of the principal sources of *joyful goodness* pursued on behalf of an ideal end. God conferred greatness on Abraham because of his humility. "I set My love upon you because even when I grant you greatness you make yourselves small [i.e. humble] before Me. I gave greatness to Abraham, and he said 'Behold, I am dust and ashes.' (Genesis 18:27)"[22] God, of course, meant genuine humility. Ironically, Martin Luther modestly boasted of being imperfect while insisting that he was always right.[23]

All religions urge cultivation of "internal friends," e.g. love and forgiveness. If you love others, you'll be rewarded with self-love. Do not cultivate "internal enemies" such as hate and anger. You'll not be punished for your hate and anger: you'll be punished *by* your hate and anger.

Compassion is another source of joyful goodness. The greatest danger is losing your compassion for your enemy, warns a Chinese saying. Compassionate de-centering is the ultimate self-centering, and it is urged by all religions, not just for fellow humans, but also for all creatures.

> The Messenger of God said: "'While a man was walking on the road, his thirst grew strong and he found a well and descended into it and drank and was leaving, when he saw a dog hanging out its tongue and licking the ground from thirst, and the man said, 'This dog's thirst is like the thirst I had,' and he went into the well again, filled his shoe with water, and held it between his teeth (while he climbed out), and gave the dog to drink. And God approved of his act and pardoned his sins.' They said, 'What, Messenger of God, shall we be rewarded for what we do for animals?' He replied, 'Yes, There is reward on every living creature.'"[24]

By being immersed in yourself and your interests, you'll be alienated from yourself. "The more one is immersed and absorbed in something or someone other than oneself the more he really becomes *himself*,"[25] says Victor Frankl. By riding others, you may get to wealth and power, but not joyful serenity; you get there by carrying others. Carrying others is not a totally altruistic endeavor.

> A farmer whose corn always took the prize at the state fair had a habit of sharing his best corn seeds with all of the farmers in the neighborhood. When asked why, he said it is really a matter of self-interest; the wind picks up the pollen and carries it from field to field. So if my neighbors grow inferior corn, the cross pollination brings down the quality of my corn.

Optimism (positivism) is another source of joyful goodness. Optimism and pessimism are both attitudes about the future. Neither disposition is necessarily based on some knowledge or is capable of predicting the future. Nevertheless, people still react with powerful convictions, either with a hopeless and fatalistic attitude or a hopeful and cheerful one. A pessimist will sit at the top of a well and stare hopelessly at its bottom. An optimist can be thrown into the bottom of a well, but will keep looking up at the skies.

Pessimism and optimism are recalcitrant convictions, if not life philosophies. Pessimists and optimists will argue whether the glass is half-empty or half-full until the water in the glass evaporates. This can get even funnier: A pessimist says: 'Things are so bad; they cannot get any worse.' An optimist smiles and says, "Oh, yes they can!' A sense of humor is an important ingredient of optimism.

Both positive and optimistic attitudes are either those we are born with or cultivated by learning to be grateful. You can begin your day, almost like a daily mantra, by expressing your gratitude about something in our life. The best prayer is 'thank you:' 'I am most grateful.' You may ask when you experience a major loss, "How can you be positive about anything?" Well, the answer lies in appreciating what you still do have: your eyes, your ears. We can be grateful for being able to see, to hear, or even being able to express our disappointments about what we have lost. The Bible emphasizes joyfulness even in all adverse conditions: "as sorrowful, yet always rejoicing; as poor, yet making many rich; as having nothing, and yet possessing all things."[26]

Simplicity is another source of joyful goodness. This is not naiveté, ignorance or simple-mindedness; in fact, it is the opposite. It is informed simplicity. It is a way of "uncomplicating" daily life that provides vital comfort. In *The Tibetan Book of Living and Dying*, such simplicity is described as "unexpectedly ordinary. . . . not something elaborate and esoteric, it is in fact profound common sense." Buddhist tradition values this "wisdom of ordinariness."[27] Simplicity has depth that exceeds all complexities.

In a Zen story:

> The disciple asked his Master: "Master, how do you put enlightenment into action?. . ."
>
> "By eating and by sleeping," replied the master. "But Master, everybody sleeps and everybody eats."
>
> "But not everybody eats when they eat, and not everybody sleeps when they sleep."[28]

A philosophy of simplicity extends to ambitions and possessions as well. Ambition is like medication: in a proper dose, it is useful, and in excess, it is poisonous. William Henry Davies has such a danger in his mind when he wrote the following stanza:

I had ambition, by which sin
The angels fell;
I climbed and, step by step, O Lord,
Ascended into Hell.[29]

Stoics offer a measured indifference or restraint: wealth and position, are *adiaphoric*—indifferent to the vicissitudes of life—and as such, they cause neither happiness nor unhappiness. Accumulation of things, or preoccupation with possessions, clutters the mind. The cult of things stunts the soul; excesses stress the body and the mind. Even a Zen master suffers from the burden of enlightenment.

Chronic appropriation, independent of needs, is a form of addiction that never leads to contentment, and there is no end to it. Gary Zukav says in the *The Seat of the Soul*, "An addiction cannot be satisfied by its object."[30] Some people want more than they *want*, rather than what they need. There is no cure for consumption. The Bible says: All the labor of man is for his mouth, and yet the appetite is not filled.[31] Such craving has the potential for moral mutation.

Wealth provides comfort, pleasure, and leisure, but potentially it can also be the tomb of the soul. There is a danger in sacrificing joyful living in the struggle for more wealth, while perpetually deferring fulfillment. "The enemy of being is having," said Karl Marx.[32] Contentment comes not by "additions" but by subtraction: having less, not more and wishing for what you already have. Not the need, but the desire (*unsipped*) is the cause of many sufferings.

We don't breathe more than we need. The spiritual philosopher Henri Bergson says, "The battle for the soul has to be buttressed not by objects but arrived at by *objectlessness*."[33]

Religious leaders, philosophers, and poets all agree that there is no satiety in owning. They do not advocate self-negating asceticism; just domesticate your yearnings. Aware of human desire to transgress, religions urge austerity of mind, body, speech, and material. If anything, the more we acquire the larger becomes our psychological emptiness, and we never arrive at a state of wholeness. As John of the Cross tells it, in order to obtain everything, you must:

Desire to possess nothing.
In order to arrive at being everything,
Desire to be nothing.[34]

Only nothing can be everything.

NOTES

1. Jeremy Bentham, *The Collected Works of Jeremy Bentham: Chrestomathia*, ed. M.J. Smith and W. H. Burston (Oxford: Clarendon Press, 1983), 8–10.

2. Daniel Haybron, "Happiness," *Stanford Encyclopedia of Philosophy* (July 2011), retrieved on July 10, 2018. http://plato.stanford.edu/entries/happiness/#Rel.

3. John Stuart Mill, "Chapter V: A Crisis in My Mental History-One Stage Onward," in *Autobiography* (Project Gutenberg EBook#10378, 2003).

4. Dalai Lama, Desmond Tutu, Douglas Abrams, *The Book of Joy* (New York: Avery, 2016), 42.

5. 1 Thessalonians 5:16.

6. *The Dhammapada*, trans. Eknath Easwaran (Berkeley, California: Nilgiri Press, 1985), 45.

7. Stephen R. Covey, *The Seven Habits of Highly Effective People: Powerful Lessons in Personal Change*, (New York: Free Press a Division of Simon and Schuster, 2004), 28.

8. John Skorupski, *Why Read Mill Today?* (New York: Routledge, 2006), 27.

9. M. Scott Peck, *The Road Less Traveled: A New Psychology of Love, Traditional Values and Spiritual Growth*, 99.

10. James Hillman, *The Myth of Analysis* (New York: Harper Perennial, 1992), 92.

11. Donna Schaper, *Stripping Down* (San Diego: LuraMedia, 1991), 7.

12. John Keats, "Lamia," in *The Complete Poems* (New York: Penguin Putnam, Inc.), 431.

13. Tenzin Gyatso, His Holiness the 14th Dalai Lama, personal communication.

14. John Skorupski, *The Domain of Reasons* (Oxford: Oxford University Press, 2010), 337–338.

15. Paul Kurtz, *Forbidden Fruit: The Ethics of Humanism* (Amherst: Prometheus Books. 1988), quoted in Victor J. Stenger, *God the Failed Hypothesis*, (Amherst: Prometheus Books, 2008), 209.

16. Solomon Asch, *Social Psychology*, (Englewood Cliffs: Prentice Hall, 1952), 378.

17. Matthew 7:12.

18. Confucius, *Confucian Analects, The Great Learning and Doctrine of Man*, trans. James Legge (New York: Dover Publications, Inc., 1971), 394.

19. Isocrates, "Nicocles or the Cyprians, Section 61" in *Isocrates, Volume I: To Demonicus. To Nicocles. Nicocles or the Cyprians. Panegyricus. To Philip. Archidamus* trans. George Norlin (Cambridge: Harvard University Press, 1928).

20. Michael Shermer, *The Science of Good and Evil*, (New York: Henry Holt and Company, LLC, 2004), 25.

21. Karen Armstrong, *The Great Transformation The Beginning of Our Religious Traditions* (New York: Anchor Books, 2007), 476.

22. *Hullin* 89a, in *Judaism,* ed. Arthur Hertzberg (New York: George Braziller, 1962), 29–30.

23. Carlos Eire, "Slaying the Dragon of the Dark Ages," Review of Martin Luther: The Man Who Rediscovered and Changed the World by Eric Metaxas (Viking), December 18, 2017, *The New York Times*: https://www.nytimes.com/2017/12/18/books/review/eric-metaxas-martin-luther.html. Retrieved July 11, 2018.

24. Muhammed Al-Bukhārī, *Kitāb al Jāmi' al Sahīh*, ed. M. Ludolf Krehl and Theodor Willem Juynboll (Leiden: Brill, 1868-1908), Vol. IV, 117.

25. Viktor E. Frankl, *The Unconscious God, Psychotherapy and Theology* (New York: Simon and Schuster, 1975), 79.

26. Corinthians 6:10.

27. Sogyal Rinpoche, *The Tibetan Book of Living and Dying*, 54.

28. Sogyal Rinpoche, *The Tibetan Book of Living and Dying*, 83.

29. William Henry Davies, "Ambition," *Ambition and Other Poems* (London: Jonathan Cape, 1929), 11.

30. Gary Zukav, *The Seat of the Soul* (New York: Fireside, 1990), 150; quoted in T. Byram Karasu, *The Art of Serenity* (New York: Simon and Schuster, 2003), 51.

31. Ecclesiastes 6:7.

32. Irving Kristol, "Corporate Capitalism in America," in *The Autobiography of an Idea: Neoconservatism: "The Enemy of Being is Having," (New York: The Free Press: A Division of Simon and Schuster, 1995), 223–224.* Retrieved on July 11, 2018 https://books.google.com/books?id=S2nUuTagIw8C&pg=PA223&dq=%22the+enemy+of+being+is+having%22+and+karl+marx&hl=en&sa=X&ved=0ahUKEwjLvvP7hJjcAhVPmeAKHTYfDxUQ6AEINDAC#v=onepage&q=%22the%20enemy%20of%20being%20is%20having%22%20and%20karl%20marx&f=false.

33. Henry Bergson, *Creative Evolution*, trans. Arthur Mitchell (New York: Henry Holt and Co., 1911), ix. (Project Gutenberg Ebook # 26163, 2008).

34. John of the Cross, "Book 1, Chapter 13, Verse 11," in *Ascent of Mount Carmel*, trans. and ed. E. Allison Peers, (Bottom Hill Publishing, 2010), 92.

Lesson Eight

Live Your Death

Come to terms with your ending, and be serene

We are all citizens of time.

We are, as all other creatures, earthbound and time-bound. Our being is a being in time. We inhabit and eventually inherit the earth. The earth is everyone's final home, where no one seems eager to go. The Roman philosopher Seneca was, at times, Stoic, believing in an inner kingdom where virtue is in harmony with *Logis*, and at times, Epicurean, adherent to the idea of death being a dissolution to new forms, and at still other times, Platonic, promoting the concept of immortality and infinite incarnation. Mostly, all at once, he represents our common dilemma: No theory of dying is satisfactory; we just don't want to die. The Bible confirms it: "Whoever wants to die, doesn't want to."[1] What is more amazing is that no one believes that he/she is going to die, in spite of incontrovertible statistical evidence against it. A person's relationship to this statistic changes only when he becomes one.

How long a life is satisfactory? Churchill, apocryphally, on being told he would live 20 years longer if he didn't drink, smoke, or eat so much, is reported to have said, 'It would only seem 20 years longer.'

As it is for tale, so it is for life: not how long life is, but how good it is. Seneca says "There's no difference between the longest and the shortest life, if you survey how long a person lived and compare it with how long he *didn't* live."[2] Even people with severe chronic pain, extreme disabilities, or terminal illness do not necessarily want to die. They want to be cured, saved and live. In Chapter 7 of *The Death of Ivan Ilyich*, Tolstoy describes Ivan Ilyich, the forty-five year-old magistrate dying in agonizing pain, as someone just wanting to be comforted, with his legs raised to ease his suffering by his empathic caretaker Gerasim, the only one to understand Ilyich's need for pity, comfort, and his yearning to live: "He wished most of all (though he would have been ashamed to confess it) for someone to pity him as a sick child is pitied. He longed to be petted and comforted. He knew he was an important functionary, that he had a beard turning grey, and that therefore what he longed for was impossible, but still he longed for it."[3]

What Ivan Ilyich longed for, as do the rest of us, is immortality, or at least some hope for incarnation. The Abrahamic religions (but less so in Judaism) offer some promise of such hope. Within Eastern religions, a Western writer presents a variation of such consolation poetically:

> Only there seeds that fall
> grow.[4]

You may have witnessed intensified manifestations of this desire to live or the fear of dying towards the very end of someone's life. There can be dramatic expressions of love or hate, last-gasp confessions, revelations, and religious conversions. Cognitively totally intact individuals uncharacteristically may succumb to profanity, inappropriate behavior, irreverence, or be cryptic and ironic. According to Benjamin Disraeli, the last words of William Pitt, a very serious stern man, who in fact served seventeen years as the Prime Minister of England were, "I think I will have one of Bellamy's veal pies."[5] This charming, perhaps apocryphal story, owes its origin to an old doorkeeper at the House of Commons.

Most people underestimate their longevity on earth and cannot believe that they are even old enough to die. Shortly before his death, Sir Isaac Newton's reportedly said, "I do not know what I may appear to the world, but to myself I seem to have been only like a boy playing on the seashore, and diverting myself in now and then finding a smoother pebble or a prettier shell than ordinary. . . ."[6] He was 85 years old.

Some people, at their last minutes, try to compose their epitaph. Mozart was trying to mouth the sounds of the timpani in *Requiem Mass* in D Minor[7] and managed to write this Requiem for himself. Others can be mysterious, and even confounding. Albert Einstein, who was determined not to speak German after he sufficiently mastered English, spoke in German on his deathbed. No one in the room knew German.[8]

Of course, the accuracy of many of these statements cannot be ascertained; some are glorified, some fabricated, and always out of context. All these anecdotes may be no more than evocative of human frailty in the face of death.

Death is perceived as a black-hole phenomenon of discontinuity, randomness, chaos, and meaninglessness, all of which nourish this frailty. We fear death and are petrified of our own disappearance. Meanwhile we don't remember the era of our pre-birth non-existence. When a well-known Zen master, while lying on his deathbed, was asked by one of his students, "How is it for you now, Master?" he replied, "Everything is fine, but my body is having a hard time."[9] For the less enlightened, the mind is also having a hard time.

There are of course, individuals like the rabbi in the following vignette who are possessed with life with *lipful* smiles and who lean forward and welcome the temporality of the world:

> There was once a young tourist, who paid a visit to a renowned Rabbi. He was amazed to see that the rabbi's house was completely empty. The tourist asked the Rabbi "where is your furniture?" "Where is yours?" the Rabbi replied. "Mine?" said the puzzled tourist. "But I am only passing through." The Rabbi smiled "So am I, son; so am I."

Since the dawn of civilization one main impetus of all religions has been to present death as not so frightening but as a desirable event, or even something to look forward to. "When told by his atheist son that there is no God and no immortality, Fyodor Pavlovich in *The Brothers Karamazov* reflects glumly, 'There's absolute nothingness, then.' But then he presses on: 'Perhaps there is just something? Anything is better than nothing.'"[10]

Our longings and/or fears notwithstanding, what happens after we die is unknowable; no one returns from death to testify.

> Once, there was a king who was equally concerned, if not a little too preoccupied. He asked the court's wise man to tell him what happens to a man after death. "How should I know, my King" the wise man replied. The king pressed: 'Well, you are the wise man of the kingdom, you should know.' The wise man replied: 'Yes, sir, but I never died!'

It is virtually impossible to conceptualize nothingness because "nothing" isn't a "something." "Nothing is simply nothing." It has no shape, no location, no essence. It is not a thing, a realm, a state, or a place. Nothingness seems to be the diametric opposite of *everythingness* in life.

That "nothingness" is disorganizing even to the most stable minds. Not only that state of "nothingness," but any change generates anxiety: we all long for sameness and forever. Even potentially benign changes generate some ambiguous unrest, as we see them within the prism of fear. Death itself is worse: it is fear-scented because dying is a final change and does not change into something else; it is a change into a void.

Armstrong says, "Human beings cannot endure emptiness and desolation; they will fill the vacuum by creating a new focus of meaning."[11] When we are confronted with the dark side of dying, with no longer being and that sense of finitude—nothingness—we will need either a religion or a philosophy that offers something in order to bear that pervasive dread. Even Hell is better than nothing, if it is eternal; of course, Heaven is preferred.

Eastern religions are philosophical; their offers are more abstract and transformational. Abrahamic religions promise concrete continuity. They consider man to be a subspecies *aeternitatis*. For Abrahamic religions, eternity is where the dead reside. Although the Torah has no concept of heaven and hell (these are to be experienced in this world only), there is some intimation of an afterlife. There is an on-going redemptive process in Jewish life that anticipates the post-apocalyptic arrival of the Messiah. "The Lord said to Moses, 'Behold, . . . people will rise up…'"[12] "Your dead shall live."[13] "Then the eyes of the blind will be opened. . . . Then the lame man will leap like a deer, and the tongue of the mute shall sing."[14]

Although, at some point the Bible asks, "If a person dies, will he go on living?"[15] Christianity is an eschatological religion. Its faith is rooted in an eternal world. In Ezekiel, God poses a question and tells the "son of man" that there is life after death:

> The hand of the Lord was upon me, and carried me out in the spirit of the Lord, and set me down in the midst of the valley which was full of bones,
>
> And caused me to pass by them round about: and, behold, there were very many in the open valley; and, lo they were very dry.
>
> And he said unto me, Son of man, can these bones live?[16]

In the Catholic faith, after death, "[the soul] survives the body and that being set free from the bars of the [present] body,"[17] and will later be united with their bodies for eternal life. "And the souls of those who have incurred no stain of sin after their Baptism, and those souls, too, who though stained have been duly purged whether with their bodies or after separation from their bodies as we mentioned above, are straightway received into heaven . . . And then the souls of those who die in actual mortal sin . . . straightway go down to hell."[18]

Islam is more specific: The righteous will go to a heaven that is filled with an abundance, and they will luxuriate "reclining on beds the linings of which are of brocade, and the fruit of the two gardens within reach to cull. (Qur'an 55:54) . . . therein are maids of modest glances whom no man nor ginn has deflowered before . . . (Qur'an 55:56) The wicked will go to hell and] broil in a blaze!" (Qur'an 84:12)[19]

No matter what you think of all the people's beliefs, you have to be careful about and not to temper with it unless you have something better to offer. Viktor Frankl recounts one such situation from his Nazi concentration camp experience:

> I shall never forget how I was roused one night by the groans of a fellow prisoner, who threw himself about in his sleep, obviously having a horrible nightmare. Since I had always been especially sorry for people who suffered from fearful dreams or deliria, I wanted to wake the poor man. Suddenly, I drew back the hand which was ready to shake him, frightened at the thing I was about to do. At that moment I became intensely conscious of the fact that no dream, no matter how horrible, could be as bad as the reality of the camp which surrounded us, and to which I was about to recall him.[20]

For non-believers, afterlife concepts of religions may seem childish, but their own yearning for eternity still exists. We all have the visceral taste of *nature's eternity*, the title of an essay by Rubert Spira, who paraphrased the French artist Paul Cézanne: 'everything vanishes and falls apart.'[21] This yearning may be best addressed by understanding the proper meaning of time and eternity. Space and time, past, present, and future are only stubbornly persistent illusions, says Einstein;[22] they are modes in which we think, not in which we live. Eternity doesn't mean endless time; it means timelessness and formlessness. It is made of a succession of moments. The present is the eternal now. Such a definition of eternity may be nostalgically sad and not emotionally satisfying, but it is true; the earth is the witness. We are here; it is now. This is it.

We, like the rest of all creatures and things, are made of time-limited organic and inorganic substances. We cease to exist in our present form: those substances will serve to make other creatures and things, and thus we will exist timelessly in many forms. Eternal life is this primordial dissolution, a silent return to an inorganic state. This is the highest understanding upon which all subsequent knowledge must depend. The Bible approximates:

All life comes from the ground, all of it goes back to the ground.[23] "The silver thread is broken, the golden bowl is shattered, the amphora at the fountain breaks, the bucket falls into the well, the earth returns to dust."[24]

A fear of death creeps in with the first signs of getting old. These signs can be as mild and superficial as the appearance of wrinkles on the face, sun spots on hands, mild drooping of upper eye lids, thinning hair, lessening of energy, weight gain and difficulty losing it, receding gum lines, and declining sexual desire.

Signs of aging accelerate, as cells in our body get older. Cells are genetically programmed to die after a finite number of divisions to make new cells. As the number of cells age and decrease in all organs, they become less and less functional. With each passing decade, degrees of early and mild signs of aging intensify; serious signs and symptoms appear, representing a continuous decline of organs and aging's associated conditions. Loss of bone density will lead to fractures; vertebral disks get thinner and cause back pain and loss of height; a thinning of cartilages of various joints creates arthritic disorders and ligament tears; decreases in muscle mass (sarcopenia) may result in increased fat tissue and loss of strength and energy.

Changes in the senses are not necessarily dramatic but no less disturbing. Optical lenses may stiffen and make it difficult to focus: needing brighter lights to see; needing glasses for near and farsightedness, not being able to discern different shades and colors. One may develop floaters, experience chronic watering eyes (due to decreasing fluid that lubricates eyes) or conversely, drier eyes. Hearing loss is common and generates social problems such as an inability to discern high-pitched sounds, especially in noisy restaurants. One may also notice a diminished ability to taste and smell, as well as an actual lengthening of the nose and drooping of its tip, resulting from less muscle tone and the pull of gravity.

The brain is more resilient, but the loss of a number of brain cells will diminish short-term memory and vocabulary, often resulting in word-finding difficulties. Kidneys become smaller, thus decreasing their capacity to remove waste products from the blood. We often, as we age, need lower doses of medications as a result. In women, ovaries shrink, and the walls of the vagina get thinner, and result in pain during intercourse. In men, decreasing blood flow to the penis and testosterone create erectile dysfunction. Aging cells generate many other dysfunctions; declining hormones, blood production, and cells of the immune system make the individual vulnerable to various diseases. This is the period where emotions reign, especially anxiety and dysphoria, which are equal-opportunity symptoms. At times, more than just dysphoria, a full-blown depression ensues.

The music of Richard Strauss and the words of Hofmannsthal sing of this with devastating delicacy:

> I remember a little girl. . .
> But how can that be. . .
> Once I was that little Resi,
> and then one day I became an old woman?
> …If God wills it so, why allow me to see it?
> Why doesn't he hide it from me?
> Everything is a mystery, such a deep mystery. . .
> I feel the fragility of things in time.
> From the bottom of my heart, I feel we should
> cling to nothing.
> Everything slips through our fingers.

All that we seek to hold on to dissolves.
Everything vanishes, like mist and dreams. . .
Time is a strange thing.
When we don't need it, it is nothing.
Then, suddenly, there is nothing else.
It is everywhere around us. Also within us.
It seeps into our faces.
It seeps into the mirror, runs through my temples. . .
Between you and me it runs silently, like an hourglass.[25]

So, given all of these signs of the "one-way street" aging and the inevitability of the ultimate outcome, our fear of dying and the anxiety associated with the process are quite natural. How does one come to terms with that, as one has no choice? Come to terms with dying. It is the last and toughest adaptive attitude—a philosophy. This may seem paradoxical but living joyfully while aging is the first step toward coming to terms with your ending peacefully. Facing death has to be tailored to your own psychological state. The ancient Greek adage that neither sun nor death can be looked at straight is absolutely true about the sun; as to death, it depends on the dying person. Some will avert their eyes as long as they can; others will look at it squarely in its face. A peaceful death rarely can be achieved towards the end of life. This eventuality has to be dealt with while we are young and healthy. Seneca wrote in *On the Shortness of Life* (7.3): "[a] whole lifetime is needed to learn how to live, and—perhaps you'll find this is more surprising—a whole lifetime is needed to learn how to die."[26] That is why, at the age of 80, Socrates advised the young to "practice dying."[27]

There is some melancholy in the ending of anything, and death has its particular flavor of sadness. Of course, dying is different for each person, for people die the way they have lived. The extreme intensity of the fear of death, that indescribable dread of no longer being, i.e., a *bad death*, is closely related to a person's not having lived fully. Our fear and preoccupation with dying deprive us of living the present in its fullest. The writer Albert Camus said, "If there is a sin against life, it consists perhaps not so much in despairing of life as in hoping for another life and eluding the implacable grandeur of this life."[28] Some operate with the idea that if you don't live, you don't have to die.

That "grandeur" of life means different things to different people. There are no objective criteria: it is how you experience your own life. Deepak Chopra with his term "qualia" emphasizes the importance of subjective experiences within a good life:

> . . . How we experience life rather than how we measure it. The word *qualia*, which is Latin for "qualities," is a tag for a world that is as far-reaching as quantum physics but points in the opposite direction, away from physical objects and toward subjective experience. Whereas quanta are "packets" of energy, qualia are the everyday qualities of existence—light, sound, color, shape, texture.[29]

A good death emerges from a good life—good qualia—the source of physical and psychological longevity. Michelangelo died at the age of eighty-nine while still working on Rondanini Pietà.[30]

Birth and death are united in rhythmicity and harmony. At any moment we are bearers of both, though we are only passive recipients of each. A. E. Housman said, "I, a stranger and afraid/ in a world I never made."[31] Similarly, paraphrasing Martin Heidegger, we are flung into a world that is not of our own making.[32] He could have added that we are *flung out of it without knowing where and why*. In his powerful memoir of the cancer that would take his life (even before he finished his book), *When Breath Becomes Air*, Paul Kalanithi quotes Sir Thomas Browne from his book *Religio Medici*, "With what strife and pains we come into the world we know not, but 'tis commonly no easy matter to get out of it."[33] Kalanithi's wife reports that her husband even asked to be buried with Browne's book.

Yes, it is not easy, but once you are no longer trapped in that illusionary immortality and once you are fully conscious of the inevitability and desirability of dying, you will, on your own volition, have flung the rest of your body into "the eternity."

To die well—death in equanimity—cannot be learned by repetition as one only dies once. So a good death can come only from cultivating some generic sense of wonder. Angels fly because they take themselves lightly. If you contemplate, you'll be astonished by our total absence prior to birth, or even just for being born. French biologist Jacques Monod says "The ancient covenant is in pieces; man at least knows that he is alone in the unfeeling immensity of the universe, out of which he emerged only by chance."[34] Embrace this "chance," and be wondrous about your potential disappearance. Transform your vulnerability, your confusion and suffering into astonishment; will it, and transform dying. We live other's deaths and die other's lives. We all miss the experience of one of the most extraordinary events of our lives, our births—our beginnings; we shouldn't miss the other, our own death—our end; that is a privilege.

Chopra soberly observes that the concept of a body clock is inevitably disturbing to the imagination: we liken it to a time bomb that is constantly ticking, while animals unknowingly await their own destiny—aging and the *death clock*.[35] That awareness, if not the preoccupation about it shortchanges the living. Not only is it a waste of time, as it does not stop the death clock, it also generates chronic anxiety. "No man can have a peaceful life who thinks too much about lengthening it," says Seneca.[36] People can live better, and maybe even longer, if they are not so preoccupied with living longer. We may expect that we will fatigue from our unrealized worries about health, work, life, or death and that our neuroses will crumble away from sheer exhaustion. Unfortunately not. In the words of E.M. Cioran, we continue to fear "to have accomplished nothing and to die overworked."[37] In fact, most likely we will have accomplished plenty but died *overworried.*

There is a Zen saying: don't fight death; fighting anything makes it into an enemy; embrace it. You'll live longer if you stop trying to live longer; you'll not fear death if you accept the transiency of life. If you realize that life is death postponed, and every day you have one day less to live, you'll be wiser to live life to its fullest. You need to love life but loosely hold on to it; dwell in it like any moment you are about to move out. That way you can let go when the time comes. You'll stop yearning for immortality and meditate on dying while you are alive and well. For Michelangelo, who experienced a religious conversion much later toward the end of his life, death was not separate, but rather, says Charles de Tolnay, "an integral part of life." Tolnay quotes Michelangelo, "If life pleases us, death, being made by the hands of the same creator, should not displease us."[38] It is in the Bible: Teach us to number our days that we may apply our hearts to wisdom.[39] Teach us to meditate on death that we might be wise.

"Death, even the hint of death has a way of making everything else trivial."[40] A group of Mullahs were in intense discussion of the religious merits of walking on the right or left side of the coffin when they carry it. Finally, not coming to an end of the argument, they consulted Mullah Nasreddin who having listened to their argument declared: 'It doesn't matter, just as long as you are not inside of it.'

The Bible says: What is life? You are a mist that is seen for a moment and then disappears.[41] If we really understand the notion of impermanence, our perspective about how we live the present will change. We can then embrace life and live our lives in complete amazement. We cannot afford to get lost in the triviality of pains and miseries of daily life, but take a philosophical, if not poetic, stand about life and death as Baron Brooke Fulke Greville had and sprinkle it with Zen dust:

> You seek what life is in death,
> Now find it air that once was breath.
> New names unknown, old names gone:
> Till time end bodies, but souls none.
> Reader! then make time, while you be,
> But steps to your eternity.[42]

Epicureans did not allow their mortality to poison their minds. They considered death as simply the extinction of consciousness. Once you really understand that "when we exist, death is not present, and when death is present we do not exist," worrying about death becomes pointless. Death becomes more acceptable and even enjoyable, not by yearning for "infinite time, but by ridding us of the desire for immortality."[43]That joy is so special in death, you may wish for eternal death. John Gray says how deadly not dying would be:

> Longing for everlasting life, humans show that they remain the death-defined animal. . . . While most people never give up dream-

ing of immortality, individuals here and there can loosen the hold of the dream on their lives. If you understand that in wanting to live forever you are trying to preserve a lifeless image of yourself, you may not want to be resurrected or to survive in a post-mortem paradise. What could be more deadly than being unable to die?[44]

In Classical mythology, Apollo, the son of Zeus offers the beautiful priestess Sibyl of Cumae, the gift of a very long life in exchange for her love. Sibyl of Cumae points to a heap of sand in a pile and asks him to give her as many years as there are sand grains in the pile (there were a thousand!) But she fails to include in her negotiation a codicil for eternal youth. So, with passing decades she becomes the prey of old age; she grows decrepit and so shrunken that she was hung on the wall of a minor priest who charged visitors to see the talking curiosity: the only thing that was audible was her yearning to die.[45] Dying at the height of one's obituary may be the only way not to regret for having lived too long.

Like Sibyl of Cumae people do not just want to live longer, in a chronically aging state; what they really want is to remain youthful. Actually, life including its youthful phase is long enough. We all, though, have our own subjective feelings of the passage of time.[46] How long is forever? Sometimes, not more than a few seconds.

It is not that we have a short span of time, but that we waste much of it, says Seneca. Live your life with zest and determination until the end.

Once upon a time, an old monastic began her pilgrimage to the holiest shrine in the highest mountain. She stopped at an inn at the foot of the mountain to ask for directions. The innkeeper tried to discourage her: 'This mountain is too high and steep, and you could not possibly climb it.' The old monastic smiled: 'I'll be climbing to the shrine, not to the mountain. You see, my heart has been there all my life. Now, it is simply a matter of taking my body there, as well.'[47]

Life may be a journey to death—our final destination. The Bible warns: Our days on earth are only a fleeting shadow.[48] This warning is definitely comforting for those who believe in God. For atheists, though, it is commonly a source of dismay and irrelevancy; at times, it is a source of odd *yearning*. Julian Barnes, in the first sentence of his 2008 memoir, a conversation with his philosopher brother, *Nothing to be Frightened Of*, says, "I don't believe in God, but I miss him."[49]

Live dying but not suffer it—health in death. Pain is certain but suffering is optional, says Buddha. This is true not only about dying, but just about everything. In fact, everything is tolerable, if there is an end to it. It is even more so about death, for it happens only once; you never have to die again! Death is certain, but living is optional, in a rewording of Buddha. Live your death. It is the final defining rite of passage. We dwell in time; that transiency, ephemerality, is what makes dying such a precious phase of life. Think of life as the foreplay for death, says Thomas Moore.[50]

Towards the end of his life, Freud added the third instinct to his previous two, i.e., sex and aggression: Thanatos—the drive to die. In ancient Greece, Thanatos (death) was the son of Nyx (night) and Chronos (time). He was also the twin brother of Hypnos (sleep). If interpreted, it means that when the time comes we would be driven by the instinct of dying, as we fall from the highest level of awareness and fade away into eternal sleep. *The brother of sleep*, Bach calls it[51], in his marvelous cantata BWV 56, "I would gladly bear the Cross." Seneca urges grace and dignity in death: "My friend Vagellius expresses it superbly in that famous poem of his: 'If fall I must, then let me fall from heaven.'"[52]

Death is the universal endpoint; it is everyone's birthright. The earth is our witness, ask your ancestors, says Moses in his final song:

> Remember the days of ages past
> Ask your father, he will inform you
> Your elders, they will tell you.[53]

NOTES

1. Epistle 117: 21–24.
2. Seneca, *How to Die: An Ancient Guide to the End of Life*, ed., trans., and introduced by James S. Romm (Princeton: Princeton University Press, 2018), 36.
3. Leo Tolstoy, *The Death of Ivan Ilyich* with an Introduction by Ronald Blythe, trans. Lynn Solotaroff (New York: Bantam Re-issue Edition, 2004), 87–88.
4. Alice O. Howell, as quoted in Thomas Moore, *Ageless Soul: The Lifelong Journey Toward Meaning and Joy* (New York, St. Martin's Press, 2017), 272.
5. Benjamin Disraeli in Robin Reilly, *Pitt the Younger* (Littlehampton Book Services Ltd., 1978), Note #620: 367.
6. Isaac Newton in Louis Trenchard More, *Isaac Newton: A Biography* (Dover Publications, 1934), 664.
7. Wolfgang Amadeus Mozart in Otto Erich Deutsch, *Mozart: A Documentary Biography* (Palo Alto: Stanford University Press, 1965), 524–525.

8. Albert Einstein in Brian O'Kill, *Exit Lines: Last Words of the Famous and Infamous* (Essex: Longman Group Limited, 1986), xii.
9. Rupert Spira, *The Nature of Consciousness: Essays on the Unity of Mind and Matter*, 127.
10. Fyodor Dostoevsky, "Part I: Book III The Sensualists Chapter VIII Over the Brandy" in *The Brothers Karamazov,* trans. Constance Garnett (New York: The Lowell Press), retrieved July 7, 2018. http://www.gutenberg.org/files/28054/28054.txt.
11. Karen Armstrong, *A History of God: The 4000-Year Quest of Judaism, Christianity, and Islam,* 399.
12. Deuteronomy 31:16.
13. Isaiah 26:19.
14. Isaiah 35:5–6.
15. Job 14:14.
16. Ezekiel 37: 1–3.
17. St. Ambrose, "On the Resurrection," in *Two Books on the Death of Satyrus* (NF2); in *Catholicism,* ed. George Brantl (New York: George Braziller, 1962), 228.
18. Council of Florence, 1415–45; in *Catholicism,* 232.
19. "The Qur'an Part II" in *Sacred Books of the East Vol. 9,* ed. Friedrich Max Müller (London: Clarendon Press, 1880), 261.
20. Victor Frankl, "Experiences in a Concentration Camp," in *Man's Search for Meaning: An Introduction to Logotherapy*, 41.
21. Rupert Spira, "Nature's Eternity," in *The Transparency of Things: Contemplating the Nature of Experience*, (Oakland, California: Sahaja Publications, A co-publication with New Harbinger Publications, 2016), 145–155.
22. K.C. Cole. "Time, Space Obsolete in New View of Universe," *Los Angeles Times,* November 16, 1999. Retrieved July 11, 2018. http://articles.latimes.com/1999/nov/16/news/mn-34060.
23. Ecclesiastes 3:20.
24. Ecclesiastes 12:6–7.

25. Hugo von Hofmannstahl, *Der Rosenkavalier*, act I.

26. Seneca, *How to Die: An Ancient Guide to the End of Life*, xx.

27. Plato, *Phaedo,* Translated by Benjamin Jowett, retrieved January 21, 2017 from classics.mit.edu (360 B.C.)

28. Albert Camus, "Summer in Algiers," in *The Myth of Sisyphus and Other Essays* (New York: Vintage Books, 1991), 153.

29. Deepak Chopra and Menas Kafatos, *You Are the Universe* (New York: Harmony Books, 2017), 213–214.

30. Michelangelo and The Pietà, retrieved July 11, 2018. https://www.milanocastello.it/en/content/michelangelo.

31. Alfred Edward Housman, *Complete Poems* (New York: Henry Holt and Co.), 111.

32. Martin Heidegger, *Being and Time*, trans. John Macquarrie and Edward Robinson (New York: HarperPerennial, ModernThought, 2008), 236.

33. Paul Kalanithi, *When Breath Becomes Air* (New York: Penguin Random House, 2016), xvi.

34. Jacques Monod, *Chance and Necessity* (New York: Vintage Books, 1971), 167.

35. Deepak Chopra, *Ageless Body, Timeless Mind: the Quantum Alternative to Growing Old* (New York: Harmony Books, 1993), 161.

36. Seneca, "Epistle Four: On the Terrors of Death," in *Seneca Epistules*, trans. Richard M. Gummere (Loeb Classical Library, 1917. Reprint, Cambridge: Harvard University Press, 2002), 1–65.

37. E.M. Cioran, *Anathemas and Admirations*, trans. Richard Howard (New York: Arcade, 1991), 85.

38. Charles De Tolnay, "Michelangelo's Philosophy," in *The Art and Thought of Michelangelo,* trans. Nan Buranelli, (New York: Pantheon Books, A Division of Random House, 1964), 54, and Note #37, 129.

39. Psalm 90: 12.

40. Aristides, "Life and Letters: Nicely out of It," *American Scholar*, 62 (1993): 487–496.

41. James 4:14.

42. Baron Brooke Fulke Greville, Caelica 83, retrieved June 29, 2018. https://www.poetryfoundation.org/poems/56367/caelica-83-you-that-seek-what-life-is-in-death.

43. Epicurus, *Letter to Menoeceus* 125, in Anthony Gottlieb, *Dream of Reason: A History of Philosophy from the Greeks to the Renaissance* (London: W.W. Norton and Company, Ltd., 2000), 296.

44. John Gray, *The Immortalization Commission: Science and the Strange Quest to Cheat Death* (New York: Crown Publishers, 2012), 235–236.

45. Sibyl story: Andrzej Szczeklik, *Catharsis: On the Art of Medicine.* (Chicago: The University of Chicago Press, 2005), 26. Retrieved July 11, 2018. https://books.google.com/books?id=cKEeTdE-UVoC&pg=PA26&lpg=PA26&dq=sibyl+of+cumae+and+request+for+long+life&source=bl&ots=pPR0DflfBm&sig=72k0cn6fkQtMmUW1FpzsR1g8Tjs&hl=en&sa=X&ved=0ahUKEwjuz6O9lJjcAhVPmuAKHXunBLwQ6AEIhQEwDg#v=onepage&q=sibyl%20of%20cumae%20and%20request%20for%20long%20life&f=false.

46. Valtteri Arstila, "Time Slows Down During Accidents," *Frontiers in Psychology*, 3: Article 196(2012): 1–10.

47. Adapted from Sr. Joan Chittister's lecture, retrieved June 29, 2018. https://philipchircop.wordpress.com/tag/joan-chittister.

48. Job 8:9.

49. Julian Barnes, *Nothing to be Frightened Of* (New York: Vintage International/Vintage Books, A Division of Random House, Inc.), 3.

50. Thomas Moore, *Ageless Soul: The Lifelong Journey Toward Meaning and Joy* (New York, St. Martin's Press, 2017), 103–105.

51. Johann Sebastian Bach *Cantata BWV 56:* "Ich will den Kreuzstab gerne tragen" ("I would gladly bear the Cross"), Retrieved July 11, 2018. http://www.emmanuelmusic.org/notes_translations/translations_cantata/t_bwv056.htm.

52. Seneca, *How to Die: An Ancient Guide to the End of Life*, 115.

53. Deuteronomy 32:7.

Bibliography

Achenbach, Joel "Homeward Bound." In *Here Lies My Heart: Essays on Why We Marry, Why We Don't, and What We Find There*, edited by Deborah Chasman and Catherine Jhee, 50–56. Boston: Beacon Press, 1999.

Al-Bukhārī, Muhammed. *Kitāb al Jāmi' al Sahīh*, edited by M. Ludolf Krehl and Theodor Willem Juynboll. Vol. IV. Leiden: Brill, 1868–1908.

Anders, Guenther. "Kafka: Ritual Without Religion: The Modern Intellectual's Shamefaced Atheism." *Commentary* 8 (1949): 560–569.

Archbishop Rowan Williams. "Raymond Williams Lecture." Hay Festival, Wales, UK, June 1, 2002.

Aristides. "Life and Letters: Nicely out of it." *American Scholar*, 62 (1993): 487–496.

Armstrong, Karen. *A History of God: The 4,000-Year Quest of Judaism, Christianity, and Islam*. New York: Ballantine Books, 1993.

Armstrong, Karen. *The Great Transformation The Beginning of Our Religious Traditions*. New York: Anchor Books, 2007.

Arstila, Valtteri. "Time Slows Down During Accidents." *Frontiers in Psychology*, 3: Article 196(2012): 1–10.

Asch, Solomon. *Social Psychology*. Englewood Cliffs: Prentice Hall, 1952.

Astrow, A., C. Pulchalski, D Sulmasy. "Religion, spirituality, and health care: Social, ethical, and practical considerations," *American Journal of Medicine* 110 (2001): 283–287.

Auden, W. H. and Louis Kronenberger, ed. *Aphorisms*. New York, Dorset Press, 1981.

Bacon, Francis. *The Philosophical Works of Francis Bacon*, edited by. J.M. Robertson. New York: E.P. Dutton & Co., 1905.

Ban Breathnach, Sarah. *Simple Abundance: A Daybook of Comfort and Joy*. Sydney: Hodder Headline Australia, 2002.

Barnes, Julian. *Nothing to be Frightened Of.* New York: Vintage International/Vintage Books, A Division of Random House, Inc.

Baron Brooke Fulke Greville, Caelica 83, retrieved June 29, 2018. https://www.poetryfoundation.org/poems/56367/caelica-83-you-that-seek-what-life- is-in-death.

Barrett, William. *Irrational Man*. New York: Doubleday, 1962.

Benson, Herbert. *Timeless Healing: the Power and Belief with Marg Stark*. New York: Simon and Schuster, 1997.

Bentham, Jeremy. *The Collected Works of Jeremy Bentham: Chrestomathia*, edited by M.J. Smith and W. H. Burston. Oxford: Clarendon Press, 1983.

Berger, Peter L. *A Far Glory*. New York: Macmillan, 1992.

Bergson, Henry. *Creative Evolution*. Translated by Arthur Mitchell. New York: Henry Holt and Co., 1911. Project Gutenberg Ebook # 26163, 2008.

Blake, William. The Complete Poetry and Prose of William Blake, edited by David V. Erdman. New York: Anchor Books, 1988.

Boszormenyi-Nagy, Ivan and Barbara R. Krasner. *Between Give and Take: A Clinical Guide to Contextual Therapy*. New York: Brunnel/Mazel, 1986.

Bourdillon, Francis William. *The Night Has A Thousand Eyes and Other Poems*. Cambridge: Little, Brown, and Company, 1899.

Brantl, George, ed. *Catholicism*. New York: George Braziller, 1962.

Brussat, Frederic and Mary Ann Brussat. *Spiritual Literacy: Reading the Sacred in Everyday Life*. New York: Touchstone, 1996.

Bulfinch, Thomas. *Bullfinch's Mythology*. New York: Penguin Group, 2014.

Campbell, Joseph and Bill Moyers. *The Power of Myth*, edited by Betty Sue Flowers. New York: Doubleday, 1988.

Camus, Albert. *The Myth of Sisyphus and Other Essays*. New York: Vintage Books, 1991.

Carlyle, Thomas. *Past and Present*. Boston: Standard Publishing Company, 1898.

Carroll, Lewis. *Alice's Adventures in Wonderland and Through the Looking-Glass With introductions by Will Self and Zadie Smith*. New York: Bloomsbury, 2003.

Carus, Titus Lucretius. *On the Nature of Things*. Translated by Martin Ferguson Smith. Indianapolis: Hackett Publishing Company, Inc., 2001.

Chalmers, Randolf C. and John A. Irving, ed. *The Meaning of Life in Five Great Religions*. Toronto: Ryerson Press, 1965.

Chavkin, Allan, ed. *Conversations with John Gardner*. Jackson: University of Mississippi, 1990.

Chopra, Deepak and Menas Kafatos. *You Are the Universe*. New York: Harmony Books, 2017.

Chopra, Deepak. *Ageless Body, Timeless Mind: the Quantum Alternative to Growing Old*. New York: Harmony Books, 1993.

Cioran, E.M. *Anathemas and Admirations*. Translated by Richard Howard. New York: Arcade, 1991.

Confucius. *Confucian Analects, The Great Learning and Doctrine of Man*. Translated by James Legge. New York: Dover Publications, Inc., 1971.

Connolly, Cyril. *The Unquiet Grave: A Word Cycle by Palinarus Revised Edition with an Introduction by Cyril Connolly*. Read Books Ltd., 2013. Google Play Books Edition. Cottingham, John. *The Meaning of Life*. London: Routledge, 2003.

Covey, Stephen R. *The Seven Habits of Highly Effective People: Powerful Lessons in Personal Change*. New York: Free Press a Division of Simon and Schuster, 2004.

Cowan, Caroline Pape and Philip A. Cowan. *When Partners Become Parents: The Big Life Change for Couples*. New York: HarperCollins, 1992.

Coward, Noël. *Private Lives: An Intimate Comedy*. New York: Samuel French, Inc., 1975.

Crane, Tim. *The Meaning of Belief: Religion from an Atheist's Point of View*. London, Harvard University Press, 2017.

Darlington, Roger. "A Sense of a Goose." Retrieved July 11, 2018. http://www.rogerdarlington.me.uk/stories.html.

Davies, William Henry. "Ambition." *Ambition and Other Poems*. London: Jonathan Cape, 1929.

Dawkins, Richard. *River out of Eden: A Darwinian View of Life*. New York: Basic Books, 1995.

———. *The God Delusion*. London: Bantam, 2006.

De La Rochefoucauld, Francois Duc. *Reflections: or Sentences and Moral Maxims*. Translated from the Editions of 1678 and 1827 by J.W. Bund and J. Hain Friswell. London: Simpson Low, Son, and Marston, 188, Fleet Street, 1871. Retrieved on July 8, 2018. http://www.gutenberg.org/files/9105/9105-h/9105-h.htm.

De Lubac, Henri. *The Drama of Atheist Humanism*. Translated by Edith M. Riley. New York: Sheed &Ward, 1950.

De Mello, Anthony. *Heart of the Enlightened: A Book of Story Meditations*. New York: Doubleday, 1991.

———. *The Heart of the Enlightened*. New York: Doubleday, 1989.

De Tolnay, Charles. "Michelangelo's Philosophy." In *The Art and Thought of Michelangelo*. Translated by Nan Buranelli. New York: Pantheon Books, A Division of Random House, 1964.

De Vries, Peter. *Reuben, Reuben*. New York: Little, Brown, 1964.

Dennon, Lester E., ed. *The Basic Writings of Bertrand Russell, 1903–1959*. New York: A Clarion Book, Simon & Schuster, 1967.

Deutsch, Helene. *Confrontations with Myself*. New York: W.W. Norton and Co, 1973.

Deutsch, Otto Erich. *Mozart: A Documentary Biography*. Palo Alto: Stanford University Press, 1965.

Dicks, Henry. *Marital Tensions: Clinical Studies towards a Psychological Theory of Interaction*. New York: Basic Books, 1967.

Dostoevsky, Fyodor. *The Brothers Karamazov*. Translated by Constance Garnett. New York: The Lowell Press, retrieved July 7, 2018. http://www.gutenberg.org/files/28054/28054.txt.

Dowling, Colette. *The Cinderella Complex: Women's Hidden Fear of Independence*. New York: Summit Books, 1981.

Durkheim, Émile. *The Elementary Forms of Religious Life*. 1912; repr., Oxford: Oxford University Press, 2001.

Dworkin, Ronald. *Religion Without God*. Cambridge: Harvard University Press, 2013.

Eckhart, Meister. *Meister Eckhart: The Essential Sermons, Commentaries, Treatises, and Defense*. Translated by Edmund Colledge and Bernard McGinn. New York: Paulist Press, 1981.

Ehrenreich, Barbara. "Why It Might Be Worth It (to Have an Affair)." In *Here Lies My Heart: Essays on Why We Marry, Why We Don't, and What We Find There*, edited by Deborah Chasman and Catherine Jhee, 6–8. Boston: Beacon Press, 1999.

Eire, Carlos. "Slaying the Dragon of the Dark Ages," Review of Martin Luther: The Man Who Rediscovered and Changed the World by Eric Metaxas (Viking), December 18, 2017, The New York Times: https://www.nytimes.com/2017/12/18/books/review/eric-metaxas-martin-luther.html. Retrieved July 11, 2018.

Epictetus. "See Things for What They Are." In *The Art of Living: The Classical Manual on Virtue, Happiness, and Effectiveness A New Interpretation by Sharon Lebell*. New York: HarperOne, An Imprint of Harper Collins/Publishers, 1994.

Erikson, EH and JM Erikson. *The Life Cycle Completed: Extended Version*. New York: Norton, 1997.

Erikson, Erik. *Identity and the Life Cycle*. New York: International Universities Press, 1968.

Feuerbach, Ludwig. *The Essence of Christianity*. Translated by George Eliot. London: John Chapman, 1890.

Fisher, Helen E. *Anatomy of Love: The Natural History of Monogamy, Adultery, and Divorce*. New York: Norton, 1992.

Fox, Matthew W. *The Coming of the Cosmic Christ*. San Francisco: HarperCollins, 1988.

Frankl, Victor E. *Man's Search for Meaning: An Introduction to Logotherapy*. Cutchogue, NY: Buccaneer Books, Inc., 1992.

———. *The Unconscious God: Psychotherapy and Theology*. New York: Simon & Schuster, 1975.

Freud, Sigmund. "Leonardo da Vinci and a Memory of His Childhood." In *The Freud Reader*, edited by Peter Gay. New York, NY: W.W. Norton and Company, Inc., 1989.

———. "The Future of an Illusion." In *The Standard Edition of the Complete Psychological Works of Sigmund Freud Volume XXI*. Translated and edited by James Strachey, in collaboration with Anna Freud, Alix Strachey and Alan Tyson. London: The Hogarth Press, 1968.

———. *New Introductory Lectures on Psychoanalysis*. Translated and edited by James Strachey. New York: W.W. Norton & Company, Inc., 1965.

Friedan, Betty. *The Feminine Mystique with an Introduction by Anna Quindlen*. New York: Norton, 2001.

Gibran, Khalil. *The Prophet*. Oxford: Benedictine Classics, 2013.

Gil Fronsdal, "The Buddha's Teachings on Love," retrieved July 11, 2018. https://www.insightmeditationcenter.org/books-articles/articles/the-buddhas-teachings-on-love/.

Glantz, Kalman and John K. Pearce, *Exiles from Eden: Psychotherapy from an Evolutionary Perspective*. New York: Norton, 1990.

Godwin, Peter. "The Way We Live Now: 7-25-99; Happily Ever After." *New York Times*, July 25, 1999, Sunday Magazine Desk, Section 6, 13.

Godwin, William and Mary Wollstonecraft. *Goodwin & Mary*, edited by R.M. Wardle. Lawrence: Bison Books, 1977.

Gottlieb, Anthony. *Dream of Reason: A History of Philosophy from the Greeks to the Renaissance*. London: W.W. Norton and Company, Ltd., 2000.

Gottman, John M. and Nan Silver. *Seven Principles for Making Marriage Work*. New York: Three Rivers Press, 1999.

Gracian, Baltasar. *The Art of Worldly Wisdom: A Pocket Oracle*. Translated by Christopher Maurer. New York: Doubleday, 1992.

Gray, John. *The Immortalization Commission: Science and the Strange Quest to Cheat Death*. New York: Crown Publishers, 2012.

Grayling, A.C. *Against All Odds*. London: Oberon Books, 2007.

Hamer, Dean. *The God Gene: How Faith is Hardwired into Our Genes*. New York: Random House, 2004.

Havens, Leston. *Coming to Life*. Cambridge: Harvard University Press, 1993.

Haybron, Daniel. "Happiness," Stanford Encyclopedia of Philosophy (July 2011), retrieved on July 10, 2018. http://plato.stanford.edu/entries/happiness/#Rel.

Hazan, Cindy and Debra Zeifman "Sex and the Psychological Tether." In *Attachment Processes in Adulthood, Vol 5, Advances in Personal Relationships*, edited by Kim Bartholomew and Daniel Perlman, 151–78. London: Jessica Kingsley, 1994.

Hebbel, Christian Friedrich. "Tändelei." *In Sämtliche Werke, Bande II*. Emil Vollmer Verlag, Essen, no year given.

Heidegger, Martin. *Being and Time*. Translated by John Macquarrie and Edward Robinson. New York: HarperPerennial, ModernThought, 2008.

Heimel, Cynthia. "Beware of Mr. Right." In *Here Lies My Heart: Essays on Why We Marry, Why We Don't, and What We Find There*, edited by Deborah Chasman and Catherine Jhee, 17–21. Boston: Beacon Press, 1999.

Hertzberg, Arthur, ed. *Judaism*. New York: George Braziller, 1962.

Heyn, Dalma. *Marriage Shock: The Transformation of Women into Wives*. New York: Random House, 1997.

Hillman, James. *The Myth of Analysis*. New York: Harper Perennial, 1992.

Hoagland, Edward. "Strange Perfume." In *Here Lies My Heart: Essays on Why We Marry, Why We Don't and What We Find There*, edited by Deborah Chasman and Catherine Jhee. Boston: Beacon Press, 1999.

Horstmann, Rolf-Peter and Judith Norman, ed. *Friedrich Nietzsche, Beyond Good and Evil: Prelude to a Philosophy of the Future*, trans. Judith Norman. New York: Cambridge University Press, 2002.

Housman, Alfred Edward. *Complete Poems*. New York: Henry Holt and Co.

Howe, John R. *The Road Within: True Stories of Transformation*, edited by Sean O'Reilly, James O'Reilly, and Tim O'Reilly. San Francisco: O'Reilly and Associates, 1997. https://abuaminaelias.com/dailyhadith online/2012/11/17/hadith-on-reliance-trust-in-allah-but-tie-your-camel -and-give-regard-to-worldly-causes.

Hugo von Hofmannstahl, Der Rosenkavalier, act I.

Hung, Melissa. "Walking in Their Footsteps at a Former Japanese Internment Camp." National Public Radio. April 29, 2017, retrieved on July 11, 2018. https://www.npr.org/sections/codeswitch/2017/04/29/ 485574562/walking-in-their-footsteps-at-a-former-japanese-intern ment-camp.

Isocrates. "Nicocles or the Cyprians, Section 61." In *Isocrates, Volume I: To Demonicus. To Nicocles. Nicocles or the Cyprians. Panegyricus. To Philip. Archidamus*. Translated by George Norlin. Cambridge: Harvard University Press, 1928.

James, William. *The Varieties of Religious Experience*. New York: Longmans, Green, and Co. 1902.

John of the Cross. "Book 1, Chapter 13, Verse 11." In *Ascent of Mount Carmel*, translated and edited by E. Allison Peers. Bottom Hill Publishing, 2010.

Johnson, Samuel and Peter Peterson, ed. *Johnson's Life of Pope*. London: Macmillan and Co., Limited 1899.

Jones, Ernest. *Sigmund, Life and Work. Vol. 2, Years of Maturity, 1901–1919*. London: Hogarth Press, 1967.

K.C. Cole. "Time, Space Obsolete in New View of Universe," Los Angeles Times, November 16, 1999. Retrieved July 11, 2018. http://articles.latimes.com/1999/nov/16/news/mn-34060.

Kalanithi, Paul. *When Breath Becomes Air*. New York: Penguin Random House, 2016.

Karasu, Sylvia R. and T. Byram Karasu. *The Art of Marriage Maintenance*. New York: Jason Aronson, 2005.

Karasu, T. Byram. "Of God and Psychotherapy." *American Journal of Psychotherapy* 69(4): 357–360, 2015.

———. *The Art of Serenity*. New York: Simon and Schuster, 2003.

Kaufman, Walter, ed. *Religion from Tolstoy to Camus* with a new introduction by Paul Gottfried, Introduction. London: Routledge: Taylor & Francis Group, 1994.

Keats, John. "Lamia." In *The Complete Poems*. New York: Penguin Putnam, Inc.

Keller, Helen. *The Story of My Life With an Introduction by Jim Knipfel*. New York: Penguin Putnam, 1988.

Kierkegaard, Søren. "Our Duty to Love Those We See." In *Works of Love*. Translated by Howard and Edna Hong. New York: HarperPerennial/ModernThought, 2009.

———. *The Essential Kierkegaard*, edited by Howard V. Hong, and Edna H. Hong. Princeton, NJ: Princeton University Press, 2000.

Kipnis, Laura. *Against Love: A Polemic*. New York: Pantheon, 2003.

Kovel, Joel. *History and Spirit: An Inquiry into the Philosophy of Liberation*. Boston: Beacon Press, 1991), 221.

Kramer, Peter. *Should You Leave?* New York: Penguin, 1999.

Kristol, Irving. "Corporate Capitalism in America." In *The Autobiography of an Idea: Neoconservatism: "The Enemy of Being is Having*." New York: The Free Press: A Division of Simon and Schuster, 1995. Retrieved on July 11, 2018 https://books.google.com/books?id=S2nUuTagIw8C&pg=PA223&dq=%22the+enemy+of+being+is+h

aving%22+and+karl+marx&hl=en&sa=X&ved=0ahUKEwjLvvP7hJjcAhVPmeAKHTYfDxUQ6AEINDAC#v=onepage&q=%22the%20enemy%20of%20being%20is%20having%22%20and%20karl%20marx&f=false.

Kubie, Lawrence S. "Psychoanalysis and Marriage: Practical and Theoretical Issues." In *Neurotic Interaction in Marriage*, edited by Victor W. Eisenstein, 10–43. New York: Basic Books, 1956.

Kushner, Harold. *When Bad Things Happen to Good People*. New York: Avon Books, 1981.

Kushner, Harold. *Who Needs God*. New York: Pocket Books, 1991.

Laing, R.D. *The Politics of Experience*. New York: Pantheon, 1967.

Lama, Dalai, Desmond Tutu and Douglas Abrams. *The Book of Joy*. New York: Avery, 2016.

Larkin, Philip. "Aubade." In *Collected Poems*, edited by Anthony Thwaite. London: Faber and Faber, 2003.

Lawrence, D.H. "Glimpses." In *The Complete Poems of D.H. Lawrence*. Hertfordshire: Wordsworth Editions Limited, 2002.

Leo Tolstoy, The Death of Ivan Ilyich with an Introduction by Ronald Blythe, trans. Lynn Solotaroff (New York: Bantam Re-issue Edition, 2004), 87–88.

Levi, Primo. *The Mirror Maker*. Schocken Books, 1998.

Lucien Price, ed. *Dialogues of Alfred North Whitehead*. Boston: Little, Brown, 1954.

Luzzatto, Moses H. *Mesillat Yesharim*. Translated by Mordecai M. Kaplan. Philadelphia: Jewish Publication Society, 2010.

Maher, Bill. "Real Time with Bill Maher." HBO, February 27, 2004. Television program.

Malraux, André. *Anti-Memoirs*. Translated by Terence Kilmartin. New York: Henry Holt and Company, 1990.

Marx, Karl. "A Contribution to the Critique of Hegel's Philosophy of Right." In *Deutsch-Französische Jahrbücher*, February 1844, Marxists Internet Archive, retrieved June 29, 2018. https://www.marxists.org/archive/marx/works/1843/critique-hpr/intro.htm.

———. "Introduction to a Contribution to the Critique of Hegel's Philosophy of Right." In *Deutsch-Französische Jahrbucher*, February, 1844. Marxist Internet Archive, retrieved June 29, 2018. https://www.marxists.org/archive/marx/works/1843/critique-hpr/intro.htm.

Maushart, Susan. *Wifework: What Marriage Really Means for Women*. New York: Bloomsbury, 2001.

McGrath, Alister. *The Twilight of Atheism*. New York: Doubleday, 2006.

Michelangelo and The Pietà, retrieved July 11, 2018. https://www.milanocastello.it/en/content/michelangelo.

Mill, John Stuart. "Chapter V: A Crisis in My Mental History-One Stage Onward." In *Autobiography*. Project Gutenberg EB-ook#10378, 2003.

Miller, Michael V. *Intimate Terrorism: The Crisis of Love in an Age of Disillusion*. New York: Norton, 1995.

Monod, Jacques. *Chance and Necessity*. New York: Vintage Books, 1971.

Moore, Thomas. A Religion of One's Own: A Guide to Creating a Personal Spirituality in a Secular World (New York: Gotham Books/Penguin, 2014), 242.

———. *Ageless Soul: The Lifelong Journey Toward Meaning and Joy*. New York, St. Martin's Press, 2017.

———. *Care of the Soul*. New York: Harper Perennial, 2016. Retrieved July 11, 2018. https://www.amazon.com/Care-Soul-Twenty-fifth-Anniversary Cultivatingebook/dp/B01AFYCPMG/ref=sr_1_1_atc_badge_A28VFQ2RQJP1YP_twi_kin_2?ie=UTF8&qid=1531344681&sr=81&keywords=care+of+the+soul+by+thomas+moore#reader_B01AFYCPMG

———. *Original Self: Living with Paradox and Authenticity*. New York: HarperCollins, 2000.

———. *Soulmates: Honoring the Mysteries of Love and Relationship*. New York: Harper-Collins, 1994.

More, Louis Trenchard. *Isaac Newton: A Biography*. Dover Publications, 1934.

Moser, Benjamin. "Patriarch and Pariah." Review of American Crucifixion The Murder of Joseph Smith and the Fate of the Mormon Church, by Alex Beam, *The New York Times Book Review*, July 6, 2014: https://www.nytimes.com/2014/07/06/books/review/american-crucifixion-by-alex-beam.html.

Müller, Friedrich Max, ed. "The Qur'an Part II." In *Sacred Books of the East Vol. 9*. London: Clarendon Press, 1880.

Muller, Wayne. *Legacy of the Heart The Spiritual Advantages of a Painful Childhood*. New York: Fireside Book, 1993.

Murray, Sandra L. and John G. Holmes. "A Leap of Faith? Positive Illusions in Romantic Relationships." *Personality and Social Psychology Bulletin* 23 (6) (June 1997): 586–604.

———. "The (Mental) Ties That Bind: Cognitive Structures That Predict Relationship Resilience." *Journal of Personality and Social Psychology* 77 (6) (1999): 1228–44.

Newberg, Andrew. *Neurotheology How Science Can Enlighten Us About Spirituality*. New York: Columbia University Press, 2018.

Nietzsche, Friedrich. *The Gay Science*, edited by Bernard Williams. Translated by Josefine Nauckhoff. New York: Cambridge University Press, 2001.

———. *Thus Spake Zarathustra: A Book for All And None*. Translated by Alexander Tille. New York: The MacMillan Company, 1896.

Nock, Stephen. "The Problem with Marriage." *Society 36* (5) (1999): 20–27.

O'Brian, Patrick. *Picasso: A Biography*. New York: W. W. Norton and Co., 1976.

O'Kill, Brian. *Exit Lines: Last Words of the Famous and Infamous*. Essex: Longman Group Limited, 1986.

Pang, Alex Soojung-Kim. *Rest*. New York: Basic Books, 2016.

Paul, Pamela. *The Starter Marriage and the Future of Matrimony*. New York: Random House, 2002.

Pindar. *The Odes of Pindar*. Translated by Cecil M. Bowra. Harmondsworth: Penguin Classics, 1969.

Plato. "Book VI." In *The Republic*, with an Introduction and Notes by Elizabeth Watson Scharffenberger and Editorial Director George Stade, 190–223. Translated by Benjamin Jowett. New York: Barnes and Noble Classics, 2004.

———. *Phaedo*. Translated by Benjamin Jowett. retrieved January 21, 2017 from classics.mit.edu.

Rawson, Hugh and Margaret Miner, ed. "Theodore Roosevelt." The Oxford Dictionary of American Quotations, 2nd Edition. Retrieved July 11, 2018. http://www.oxfordreference.com/view/10.1093/acref/9780195168235.001.0001/acref-9780195168235.

Reilly, Robin. *Pitt the Younger*. Littlehampton Book Services Ltd., 1978.

Rinpoche, Sogyal. *The Tibetan Book of Living and Dying*. Edited by Patrick Gaffney and Andrew Harvey. New York: HarperCollins, 1994, 1991 reprint.

Roger Darlington's World. "Testing for Gossip, #6 (Triple Filter Test)." Last modified August 7, 2017. Retrieved June 29, 2018. http://www.rogerdarlington.me.uk./stories.html#Story50.

Rovelli, Carlo. *The Order of Time*. New York: Riverhead Books, an Imprint of Penguin Random House LLC, 2018.

Schaper, Donna. *Stripping Down*. San Diego: LuraMedia, 1991.

Schiller, David. *The Little Zen Companion*. New York: Workman Publishing 1994.

Schulweis, Harold. *Evil and the Morality of God*. Jersey City: KTAV Publishing House, 2010.

Seneca. "Epistle Four: On the Terrors of Death." In *Seneca Epistules*. Translated by Richard M. Gummere. Loeb Classical Library, 1917. Reprint, Cambridge: Harvard University Press, 2002.

———. *How to Die: An Ancient Guide to the End of Life*. Edited, translated and introduced by James S. Romm. Princeton: Princeton University Press, 2018.

Sewall, Richard Benson. *The Life of Emily Dickinson*. Cambridge, MA: Harvard University Press, 1974.

Shah, Idries. *A Perfumed Scorpion*. London: The Octagon Press, 2000.
Shermer, Michael. *The Science of Good and Evil*. New York: Henry Holt and Company, LLC, 2004.
Singer, Isaac Bashevis. "Only Small Fish Swim in Schools," Posted online by Michael Jinkins, February 20, 2018. "Isaac Bashevis Singer on the Joy of Reading." Retrieved July 10, 2018. http://www.lpts.edu/about/our-leadership/president/thinking-out-loud.
Skorupski, John. *The Domain of Reasons*. Oxford: Oxford University Press, 2010.
———. *Why Read Mill Today?* New York: Routledge, 2006.
Smith, Russell F. W. "Discussion: Linguistics in Theory—and in Practice." ETC: *Journal of Semantics* 10 (1) (Autumn 1952): 46–49.
Sontag, Susan. Review of *The Writer's Desk* by Jill Krementz. New York: Random House, 1996. Posted online by Pat Thomson, February 19, 2015. Retrieved July 10, 2018. http://world.edu/on-attention-surplus-disorder/.
Spira, Rupert. *The Nature of Consciousness Essays on the Unity of Mind and Matter*. Oxford: Sahaja Publications, 2017.
———. *The Transparency of Things: Contemplating the Nature of Experience*. Oakland, California: Sahaja Publications, A co-publication with New Harbinger Publications, 2016.
Spufford, Francis. *Unapologetic: Why, Despite Everything, Christianity Can Still Make Surprising Emotional Sense*. London: Faber and Faber, 2013.
Stenger, Victor J. *God the Failed Hypothesis*. Amherst: Prometheus Books, 2008.
Stephen G. Scholle, Billy Graham Evangelistic Association, email to author, October 13, 2003.
Swinburne, Algernon Charles. "Hymn of Man." In *The Poems of Algernon Charles Swinburne in Six Volumes, Vol. 2*, edited by John A. Walsh, 93–104. London: Chatto and Windus, 1904.
Szczeklik, Andrzej. *Catharsis: On the Art of Medicine*. Chicago: The University of Chicago Press, 2005. Retrieved July 11, 2018. https://

books.google.com/books?id=cKEeTdE-UVoC&pg=PA26&lpg=PA26&dq=sibyl+of+cumae+and+request+for+long+life&source=bl&ots=pPR0DflfBm&sig=72k0cn6fkQtMmUW1FpzsR1g8Tjs&hl=en&sa=X&ved=0ahUKEwjuz6O9lJjcAhVPmuAKHXunBLwQ6AEIhQEwDg#v=onepage&q=sibyl%20of%20cumae%20and%20request%20for%20long%20life&f=false.

Tertullian. "Chapter V. Christ Truly Lived and Died in Human Flesh: Incidents of His Human Life on Earth, and Refutation of Marcion's Docetic Parody of the Same." In *On the Flesh of Christ*. Minnesota: Lighthouse Publishing, 2015. *The Dhammapada*. Translated by Eknath Easwaran. Berkeley, California: Nilgiri Press, 1985.

Tirmidhi (reworded). *Hadith on Reliance: Trust in Allah, but Tie Your Camel*. Retrieved June 29, 2018. https://abuaminaelias.com/dailyhadithonline/2012/11/17/hadith-on-reliance-trust-in-allah-but-tie-your-camel-and-give-regard-to-wordly-causes/.

Trachtenberg, Peter. *The Casanova Complex: Compulsive Lovers and Their Women*. New York: Poseidon Press,1988.

Trevor-Roper, High. *One Hundred Letters from Hugh Trevor-Roper*, edited by Richard Davenport-Hines. Oxford: Oxford University Press, 2014.

Twain, Mark. *Mark Twain's Notebook in American Artists Edition of the Complete Works of Mark Twain*. New York: Harper and Brothers, 1935.

Tzu, Chuang. *The Complete Works of Chuang Tzu*. Translated by Burton Watson. New York: Columbia University Press, 1968.

Viorst, Judith. "A Very, Very Brief History of Marriage." In *Suddenly Sixty and Other Shocks of Life*. New York: Simon & Schuster, 2000.

Voltaire (Francois-Marie Arouet). *La Bégueule Edition augmentée*. Paris: Arvensa Éditions, 2014. E book EPUB # 9782368410035.

———. *Candide*. Translated by Lowell Blair. New York: Bantam Books, 1981.

von Goethe, Johann Wolfgang. "Book II, Chapter II." In Wilhelm Meister's *Apprenticeship and Travels, Volume I*. Translated by Thomas

Carlyle. New York: A.L. Burt, Publisher. Project Gutenberg eBook #36483, 2011.

Watts, Daniel. "Kierkegaard on Truth: One or Many?" *Mind* 127(505) (2018):197–223.

Whitehead, Alfred North. *Science and the Modern World.* 1925; repr., New York: Free Press, 1967.

Wilson, E. O. *On Human Nature.* Cambridge: Harvard University Press, 1978.

Wilson, Glenn. *The Coolidge Effect: An Evolutionary Account of Human Sexuality.* New York: William Morrow, 1982.

Winnicott, D.W. "The Capacity to be Alone." *The International Journal of Psychoanalysis* (1958), 39:416–420.

Wittgenstein, Ludwig. "Philosophical Investigations." In *Deconstruction in Context: Literature and Philosophy*, edited by Mark C. Taylor, 220–41.Chicago: University of Chicago Press, 1986.

Wright, Robert. *The Evolution of God.* New York: Back Bay Books, 2009.

Yagci, Oner. *Nasreddin Hoca Ve Fikralori.* Istanbul: Engin Yayincilik, 1994.

Zaufishan. "Iranian Poetry 'Bani Adam' Inscribed on United Nations Building Entrance," 9/17/11. Retrieved July 11, 2018. http://www.zaufishan.co.uk/2011/09/iranian-poetry-bani-adam-inscribed-on.html.

Index

About the Author

T. Byram Karasu M.D. is a Distinguished Professor Emeritus at Albert Einstein College of Medicine and Silverman Professor and University Chairman Emeritus Department of Psychiatry and Behavioral Sciences at Albert Einstein/Montefiore Medical Center. Dr. Karasu is a widely renowned psychiatrist, educator, master psychotherapist and best-selling author, whose work has been translated into many languages. Dr. Karasu has published twenty-three books, including two novels; a book of poetry; three philosophical/psychological works; a book aphorisms; and a number of psychotherapy related books.

Dr. Karasu lives and practices in Manhattan.